JOURNAL FOR THE STUDY OF THE OLD TESTAMENT SUPPLEMENT SERIES
278

Editors
David J.A. Clines
Philip R. Davies

Executive Editor
John Jarick

EUROPEAN SEMINAR IN HISTORICAL METHODOLOGY
2

Editor
Lester L. Grabbe

Sheffield Academic Press

Leading Captivity Captive

'The Exile' as History and Ideology

edited by
Lester L. Grabbe

Journal for the Study of the Old Testament
Supplement Series 278

European Seminar in Historical Methodology 2

Copyright © 1998 Sheffield Academic Press

Published by Sheffield Academic Press Ltd
Mansion House
19 Kingfield Road
Sheffield S11 9AS
England

Printed on acid-free paper in Great Britain
by Bookcraft Ltd
Midsomer Norton, Bath

British Library Cataloguing in Publication Data

A catalogue record for this book is available
from the British Library

ISBN 1 85075 907 3

CONTENTS

Part I

ARTICLES

Part II

RESPONSES

Part III

CONCLUSIONS

ABBREVIATIONS

AB	Anchor Bible
ABD	David Noel Freedman (ed.), *The Anchor Bible Dictionary* (New York: Doubleday, 1992)
AfO	*Archiv für Orientforschung*
AHw	Wolfram von Soden, *Akkadisches Handwörterbuch* (Wiesbaden: Harrassowitz, 1959–81)
AJBA	*Australian Journal of Biblical Archaeology*
ANEP	James B. Pritchard (ed.), *Ancient Near East in Pictures Relating to the Old Testament* (Princeton: Princeton University Press, 1954)
ANET	James B. Pritchard (ed.), *Ancient Near Eastern Texts Relating to the Old Testament* (Princeton: Princeton University Press, 3rd edn, 1969)
AOAT	Alter Orient und Altes Testament
BARev	*Biblical Archaeology Review*
BASOR	*Bulletin of the American Schools of Oriental Research*
Bib	*Biblica*
BibInt	*Biblical Interpretation: A Journal of Contemporary Approaches*
BJS	Brown Judaic Studies
BZAW	Beihefte zur *ZAW*
CAH	Cambridge Ancient History
CBET	Contributions to Biblical Exegesis and Theology
CBQ	*Catholic Biblical Quarterly*
FRLANT	Forschungen zur Religion und Literatur des Alten und Neuen Testaments
GAT	Grundrisse zum Alten Testament
HSM	Harvard Semitic Monographs
JAOS	*Journal of the American Oriental Society*
JBL	*Journal of Biblical Literature*
JBTh	*Jahrbuch für Biblische Theologie*
JCS	*Journal of Cuneiform Studies*
JQR	*Jewish Quarterly Review*
JQRMS	*Jewish Quarterly Review*, Monograph Series
JR	*Journal of Religion*
JRAS	*Journal of the Royal Asiatic Society*
JRE	*Journal of Religious Ethics*
JRelS	*Journal of Religious Studies*

JRH	*Journal of Religious History*
JRS	*Journal of Roman Studies*
JRT	*Journal of Religious Thought*
JSOT	*Journal for the Study of the Old Testament*
JSOTSup	*Journal for the Study of the Old Testament*, Supplement Series
JSS	*Journal of Semitic Studies*
JTS	*Journal of Theological Studies*
KAI	H. Donner and W. Röllig, *Kanaanäische und aramäische Inschriften* (3 vols.; Wiesbaden: Harrassowitz, 1962–64)
KAT	Kommentar zum Alten Testament
LCL	Loeb Classical Library
NEAE	E. Stern (ed.), *The New Encyclopaedia of Archaeological Excavations in the Holy Land* (4 vols.; Jerusalem: The Jerusalem Exploration Society, 1993)
OBO	Orbis biblicus et orientalis
Or	*Orientalia*
OTG	Old Testament Guides
OTL	Old Testament Library
PEQ	*Palestine Exploration Quarterly*
PTMS	Pittsburgh Theological Monograph Series
RlA	*Reallexikon der Assyrologie*
SANE	Sources from the Ancient Near East
SBLDS	SBL Dissertation Series
SBLMS	SBL Monograph Series
SBLSP	SBL Seminar Papers
SHANE	Studies in the History of the Ancient Near East
SJOT	*Scandinavian Journal of the Old Testament*
TCS	Texts from Cuneiform Sources
TSSI	J.C.L. Gibson, *Textbook of Syrian Semitic Inscriptions* (3 vols.; Oxford: Clarendon Press, 1971–82)
TUAT	O. Kaiser (ed.), *Texte aus der Umwelt des Alten Testaments* (Gütersloher Verlagshaus, 1982)
VAB	Vorder Asiastische Bibliothek
VT	*Vetus Testamentum*
VTSup	*Vetus Testamentum*, Supplements
WBC	Word Biblical Commentary
YNER	Yale Near Eastern Researches
ZA	*Zeitschrift für Assyriologie*
ZAW	*Zeitschrift für die alttestamentliche Wissenschaft*
ZDMG	*Zeitschrift der deutschen morgenländischen Gesellschaft*

LIST OF CONTRIBUTORS

Rainer Albertz is Professor of Old Testament at the Westfälische
Wilhelms-Universität in Münster, Germany

Hans M. Barstad is Professor of Biblical Studies at the University of
Oslo, Norway

Bob Becking is Professor of Old Testament Studies at the University of
Utrecht, The Netherlands

Robert P. Carroll is Professor of Old Testament at the University of
Glasgow, UK

Philip R. Davies is Professor of Biblical Studies at the University of
Sheffield, UK

Lester L. Grabbe is Professor of Hebrew Bible and Early Judaism at the
University of Hull, UK

Knud Jeppesen is Professor of Old Testament at the University of
Aarhus, Denmark

Thomas L. Thompson is Professor of Theology at the University of
Copenhagen, Denmark

INTRODUCTION

Lester L. Grabbe

The entity known as 'the exile' has had an extremely forceful influence on Old Testament scholarship. When discussing history and literature, things are measured in 'pre-exilic' and 'postexilic'. The concept of 'sin–exile–restoration' has made a major impact on theological thinking, both in the Old Testament itself and in subsequent theological discussion. If there is a watershed in discussions relating to the Old Testament, it is 'the exile'; the only rival is perhaps the scheme of 'pre-monarchic/monarchic' or 'pre-settlement/settlement'.

The exile is thus a powerful symbol in the Bible and in scholarship. Yet recently significant doubts have been expressed about the whole question of the exile and whether it is anything more than a literary and/or theological construct.[1] Are we dealing with a historical event or an example of virtual reality? Did real people from Judah go to Babylon into exile, only later to return and refound their temple and nation? Or are we dealing with a theological and literary concept which well served the needs of oppressed Jews, religious leaders, preachers, storytellers, theologians and writers, but was created by them from whole cloth—or at least, from some rather large off-cuts? These issues were some of the reasons why 'the exile' formed the topic for our second

---

1.   The original 'doubter' was C.C. Torrey. He questioned the exile as a concept in *Ezra Studies* (Chicago: University of Chicago Press, 1910; repr. and edited with a Prolegomenon by W.F. Stinespring; New York: Ktav, 1970), pp. 285-89, and the return in *The Chronicler's History of Israel* (New Haven: Yale University Press, 1954), pp. xxvii-xxviii. On Torrey's views, see Hans M. Barstad, *The Myth of the Empty Land: A Study in the History and Archaeology of Judah during the 'Exilic' Period* (Symbolae osloenses, 28: Oslo: Scandinavian University Press, 1996), pp. 21-23, and R.P. Carroll in his article in this volume.

meeting of the European Seminar on Methodology in Israel's History in Lausanne, 27–30 July 1997.[2]

As described in the introduction to our volume (*Can a 'History of Israel' Be Written?* European Seminar in Historical Methodology, 1[3]), the Seminar was founded to help address the current crisis over methodology in the history of ancient Israel/Palestine/Syria. The members of the Seminar (all scholars living and working in Europe) represent a spectrum of views about how (and whether) to write this history, and our first meeting showed that there is quite a range of approach even among those who are sympathetic to the radical questioning now going on in some circles.

One of the reasons for founding the Seminar was that, unfortunately, labelling and name-calling seem too often to be taking the place of proper debate. Perhaps those who originally came up with the terms 'minimalist' and 'maximalist' meant them to be neutral descriptions, but they are problematic[4] and are now often used in a polemical way. Perhaps even the term 'revisionist' was originally meant as merely descriptive, but the term 'nihilist' certainly was not.[5] If I had to describe my own position, I would naturally use the term 'moderate', but this is a self-serving designation: no doubt those of both the so-called 'minimalist' and the 'maximalist' camps would apply this word to their own positions. Those who have been called 'maximalist' are not biblical

---

2.　Another volume on 'the exile' has recently appeared: James M. Scott (ed.), *Exile: Old Testament, Jewish, and Christian Conceptions* (*Journal for the Study of Judaism*, Supplement Series, 56; Leiden: E.J. Brill, 1997). Although some of the essays in that volume (e.g. Robert Carroll's 'Deportation and Diasporic Discourses in the Prophetic Literature') relate to our concerns, the treatment of the topic by the Seminar seems to have a somewhat different aim from the volume edited by Scott. Our volume is not intended as a comprehensive treatment of the subject but rather as a collection of essays whose ultimate aim is not to study 'the exile' as such but to address questions of historical methodology.

3.　Lester L. Grabbe (ed.), *Can a 'History of Israel' Be Written?* (European Seminar in Historical Methodology, 1; JSOTSup, 245; Sheffield: Sheffield Academic Press, 1997), pp. 11-18.

4.　See the useful comments by Philip Davies, 'Introduction', in Volkmar Fritz and Philip R. Davies (eds.), *The Origins of the Ancient Israelite States* (JSOTSup, 228; Sheffield: Sheffield Academic Press, 1996), especially pp. 11-14; cf. also Grabbe (ed.), *Can a 'History of Israel' Be Written?*, p. 193.

5.　Cf. William Dever, review of *The Archaeology of Ancient Israel* (New Haven: Yale University Press, 1992), by A. Ben-Tor, in *JBL* 114 (1995), pp. 121-22.

fundamentalists,[6] and those designated 'minimalist' by some are not nihilists nor are they repudiating history, attacking biblical scholarship, nor threatening to tear asunder the entire fabric of Western civilization warp and woof. Since none of us wants our own position to be dismissed without consideration because of someone else's label, it seems only fair that we debate positions and consider arguments rather than engage in sloganizing.[7] This is one of the aims of the Seminar, and I hope that readers will agree that we are succeeding in doing this.

Of the 21 Seminar members from 9 European countries and 18 universities, approximately half were able to attend our sessions in Lausanne. The format of the meetings was a discussion around a set of questions and topics introduced by me as convener. But to inform the discussions a number of papers were circulated beforehand and served as the basis for seeking clarification on individual issues and also to suggest broader questions which needed to be addressed. These papers (often in revised form) are published here, along with several responses and my summary of and reflections on the discussion.

---

6.   This does not mean that biblical fundamentalists are not also writing on the subject; on the contrary, we all know that they are (and we also know who they are). Their arguments must also be taken into account, but because they confine themselves exclusively to a position in which the biblical text is always completely correct, their contribution can never be more than limited and can even be counter-productive. On the subject of fundamentalism see James Barr, *Fundamentalism* (London: SCM Press, 1977); Lester L. Grabbe, 'Fundamentalism and Scholarship: The Case of Daniel', in B.P. Thompson (ed.), *Scripture: Method and Meaning. Essays Presented to Anthony Tyrrell Hanson for his Seventieth Birthday* (Hull: Hull University Press, 1987), pp. 133-52.

7.   In an address at the 1997 Society of Biblical Literature meeting in San Francisco, Professor William Dever expressed some irritation at being called a 'maximalist' and, mostly recently, a 'triumphalist' (Norman K. Gottwald, 'Triumphalist versus Anti-Triumphalist Versions of Early Israel: A Response to Articles by Lemche and Dever in Volume 4 [1996]', in *Currents in Research: Biblical Studies* 5 [1997], pp. 15-42). However, after these objections, he then went on to dismiss our first volume (*Can a 'History of Israel' Be Written?*) as 'mainly negative', a manifestly inaccurate and unfair summing up, without apparently noticing that he was himself doing what he had just objected to in others. Having pointed this out at the meeting, I hope and trust that Dever's future references to the volume will be more nuanced, recognizing what our Seminar is trying to do and also the diversity of position among Seminar members, regardless of whether he agrees with any of the positions taken.

Although Hans Barstad did not produce a paper specifically for the discussion (though see pp. 120-27 below on his response to it), he had published only some months before the meeting a book directly relevant to the question, *The Myth of the Empty Land*, which also served as a part of the discussion.[8] In separate chapters he looks at earlier scholarship on the question, the biblical evidence, the archaeological evidence, the evidence from Transjordan, and the relationship between the Neo-Babylonian empire and Judah. He concludes that while there were deportations from Judah, the bulk of the population remained in the land; the archaeology shows no significant break in settlement or culture, and although there was a return, it was not nearly as large as depicted in Ezra–Nehemiah. The exile as such did not come to an end. Too much scholarly attention has been focused on the population and elite of Jerusalem.

Rainer Albertz contributed a paper on 'The Exile as an Urgent Case for Historical Reconstruction without Biblical Texts: The Neo-Babylonian Royal Inscriptions as "Primary Sources" '.[9] After discussing the difficulty of a historical reconstruction of the exilic period, he considers the character of the Babylonian royal inscriptions, noting that they exhibit their own *Tendenz*, as much as the biblical narrative. He then looks at the 'foundation myth' (*Gründungsmythos*) of the Neo-Babylonian empire, which is the view that Assyria was overthrown as punishment for Sennacherib's destruction of the Esagila temple in Babylon and the removal of the cult statue of Marduk. The policies of Nebuchadnezzar can be seen as an effort to fulfil Marduk's revenge by exalting Babylon and Marduk at the expense of the provinces. Nabonidus's removal to Haran, on the other hand, was a reversal of the process, attempting to elevate Sin to the status of imperial god. Conclusions for methodology include the following: The strong theological aim of the Nabonidus inscriptions does not mean that the events described in them are unhistorical; on the contrary, it is clear that these

8. Barstad, *The Myth of the Empty Land*. See also the earlier article of Robert P. Carroll, 'The Myth of the Empty Land', in David Jobling and Tina Pippin (eds.), *Ideological Criticism of Biblical Texts* (Semeia, 59; Atlanta: Scholars Press, 1992), pp. 79-93, to whom Barstad pays tribute. Carroll makes two points in his paper: one concerning the 'myth of the empty land' and the second, its counterpart—the 'myth of the pollution of the land' by the Canaanites.

9. He is currently writing *Die Exilszeit* (Biblische Enzyklopädie, 7; Stuttgart: W. Kohlhammer, forthcoming).

events are not invented. The 'theology of history' of these inscriptions reminds one of that in the Deuteronomistic history, the oracles against the nations, and Deutero-Isaiah. It is not sufficient to dismiss a document simply because a theological tendency has been identified in it. Furthermore, the myth is not just an interpretation of history but it also served *to shape* history; the mythical is therefore very relevant to historical enquiry. The historical (and theological) view of the Neo-Babylonian kings and our modern perspective must form a dialogue in the process of historical reconstruction.

Bob Becking highlights 'Ezra's Re-enactment of the Exile'. He surveys the sources that talk about the deportations from Judah in the early sixth century BCE. He then turns to the concept of 'return' and the picture of the book of Ezra. There are a number of problems with the narrative in Ezra, not least the relationship of the various Persian kings with the supposed events in the book. Drawing on the insights of philosophers of history, he emphasizes the fact that history writing takes the form of narrative. The narrative itself cannot be verified (since it is the creation of the historian), only the individual episodes at best. The book of Ezra is not a primary source but a narrative made up of three episodes (the return of exiled Judaeans, the abolition of the non-celebration of Passover, the story of Ezra himself). The internal construction of these three episodes differs (e.g. the first two are presented as 'return from exile' but not the third), and it is not clear what to make of these differences. The modern historian has to relate the reconstucted narrative to evidence; we do not know how the author of Ezra arrived at his narrative. The evidence for the elements in the narrative is circumstantial. Although processes like 'exile' and 'return' have taken place, we know too little to say whether the details of the book of Ezra are historically trustworthy or not.

Robert Carroll's 'Exile! What Exile? Deportation and the Discourses of Diaspora' is an *Ideologiekritik* of the concept of exile in the Hebrew Bible. Exile and exodus are two aspects of a myth which shapes much of the biblical narratives. While historical events may be reflected in these concepts, they need not be. There are too many questions without reliable answers. Determining the historicity of the return, for example, requires a decision on the relationship of Chronicles and Ezra–Nehemiah. Only one perspective is given about living in and outside the land in the literature, by and large—the perspective of the Jerusalem community and its view of itself; not everyone in the Jewish diaspora would necessarily have seen themselves as in exile. Many of these problems were recognized by C.C. Torrey whose work has yet to be properly appreciated by biblical scholarship. There is also the fact that the concept of exile and the desire for return have been a major theological metaphor in Judaism up to the present. This compounds the problem of reading the rhetoric of exile and return in the various biblical writings. However, as Torrey already pointed out, the terms 'exilic', 'pre-exilic' and 'postexilic' should be abolished from scholarly usage.

My own paper, '"The Exile" under the Theodolite: Historiography as Triangulation', recognizes the lack of data for the supposed period of exile, looking at the deportation(s) of the Northern Kingdom as well as the Southern. Instead, it tries to approach the question indirectly. An examination of the biblical sources shows a marked disparity in quality. The evidence suggests that the accounts in 2 Kings have considerable reliable information, but sources such as 2 Chronicles and Ezra are much more problematic. This means that the events leading up to the two periods of deportation can be known in some detail, though most of the sources have some form of the 'myth of the empty land'. There is very little in the way of an account of the state of the peoples in exile; however, there is some indirect evidence (Mesopotamian inscriptions on deported communities; the book of Tobit) that would allow a plausible outline (no more) to be constructed. Although there is good reason to believe that some people returned from Babylon, details are few and the data unreliable. Recognizing the theological and ideological nature of the biblical sources, a 'history' (in the sense of a critically constucted narrative) can be written of this period of history. Biblical literature, along with other sources, will be used in this reconstruction; on the other hand, the narrative will differ in essential points from the biblical narratives. This narrative would also recognize the problematic nature of continuing to use the term 'exile' as has long been conventional in scholarship.

Thomas Thompson's 'The Exile in History and Myth: A Response to Hans Barstad' is a partial extract from his forthcoming book, *The Bible and History*,[10] and his complete message will no doubt emerge much more clearly in the proper context of the complete book. As the subtitle of the article indicates, it is in part a response to Barstad's *Myth of the*

----

10. Thomas L. Thompson, *The Bible and History* (London: Cape, 1999).

Empty Land, but the emphasis is on 'response' rather than critique, for little of the paper addresses Barstad's arguments directly. Instead, Thompson has presented an alternative understanding of the data. He first considers at length the subject of exile in the ancient Near East, especially under the Assyrians. The problem is not whether there was an 'exile', for there were many; rather, we have no coherent narrative of the past from any source, whether biblical or otherwise, and are left with a fragmented and doubtful past. The main question is one of continuity—of the people, the culture and their traditions. A major problem is that there is no narrative of the exile, only of going into and returning from it. Thompson then turns to an examination of the metaphor of Jerusalem as wilderness—destruction for sin—as expressed in such writings as Nehemiah and Lamentations and also Jeremiah and Genesis. The 'exile' is Jerusalem as a moral wasteland, the emptiness of the soul without God. It is not historiography but pietism. The myth of exile and return is their myth, not modern scholarship's—and not history's.

Rather than being made up of disparate observations the three responses, as it happened, each tended to represent a fairly well-defined thesis. Therefore, these are also summarized here.

Hans Barstad discusses the 'strange fear of the Bible', an issue that has bedevilled our discussions in many ways. Recognizing that the use of the Hebrew Bible in historical reconstruction is highly uncertain, he points out that it is not a unique problem to ancient historians.[11] The same applies to Herodotus, for instance. A very useful example is that of the 'Sumerian King List', the problems of whose use are similar to those of the biblical text. For example, it was composed quite some time after the events it proposes to describe, and the text has many lacunae; it also has an ideological aim. Nevertheless, Assyriologists have found it to contain useful information about Sumerian history. The Deuteronomistic history has details about many named kings whose existence has been confirmed by extra-biblical sources; in particular, 2 Kings 24–25 on the last days of Jerusalem provides sufficient verified data to assume that it is correct in general for areas where it cannot be checked. To reject the biblical text beforehand as fictitious without due consideration is as incompatible to a scholarly

---

11. Cf. also a similar point made in Lester L. Grabbe, 'Are Historians of Ancient Palestine Fellow Creatures—Or Different Animals?', in Grabbe (ed.), *Can a 'History of Israel' Be Written?*, pp. 19-36, especially pp. 22-24.

mind as to accept it uncritically. We have to treat the Bible, for better or for worse, as we do other ancient Near Eastern sources.

Philip Davies makes several related points. The term 'exile' does not refer to an event or a fact but to an interpretation. Deportation and migration are facts, but 'exile' raises questions of identity which the historian cannot probe. Essentially, exile is something claimed about oneself or others that relates to one's identity and one's relationship to where one lives. The concept of exile operates on three levels: canonical (it closes the Former Prophets and the period of disobedience and divine anger); literary (paralleling the archetypes of creation and expulsion from paradise and mediating both punishment and salvation); and biblical historiographical (marking 'pre-exilic' and 'postexilic'). Modern scholarship has taken up the last point, leading to glorification of the monarchic period and devaluing of the postexilic period; the exilic period itself was seen as a time of intense literary activity. Using the example of his own Welsh origins, Davies points out that those who chose to return could no longer be called exiles, while those who had the chance but did not could also no longer be so called because they had a new homeland. Those who returned appropriated the name 'Judah/Israel', denying it both to those who did not return from exile and to those had not been deported in the first place. There is no question that people were deported, and some of those deportees returned. Nevertheless, the term 'exile' is not a descriptive term but an ideological one. Whether one can talk of 'returned exiles' is doubtful since we cannot know how the people who returned thought of themselves. For the historian of ancient Israel and Judah, 'exile' is a part of the colonizing rhetoric of the canonized texts. It represents a claim to be 'Israel' on the part of some groups over against other groups that had claims based on other and more reliable grounds, such as continuous occupation and biological descent. But as the elite of the province of Yehud, these colonizers did constitute the *geographical* and *political* successors of the monarchic period, which they set about describing and embellishing in their historiography. Thus, if the debate about 'exile' is a debate about historical events, those events include not only deportation and resettlement but also the imposition of certain claims over others; and the legitimacy of those claims is questionable. To that extent, the historian cannot endorse 'the exile' as a *fact* of history.

Knud Jeppesen's response raises two main issues. The first relates to the history of research on Israelite history. Even the older histories, which produced much of their history by paraphrasing the biblical text, had nothing which described the exile. Nevertheless, we can still have some story of 'the exile' to tell, at least relating to events around the fall of Jerusalem. There is no problem if it is a rather short history nor if it involves reconstruction. It is here that history and myth meet, and it involves the art of story-telling. The second point is about the exile as myth. The attempt to understand the exile as myth is very much appreciated, but the exile in myth and the exile in history also have some sort of connection. However much the exile is a reflection of myth, there are historical events underlying it. There is a dividing line between myth and history, but it is not inpenetrable; it is as legitimate to put questions of myth to history, and vice versa, as it is to put literary questions to archaeology, and vice versa.

Part I

ARTICLES

DIE EXILSZEIT ALS ERNSTFALL FÜR EINE HISTORISCHE REKONSTRUKTION OHNE BIBLISCHE TEXTE: DIE NEUBABYLONISCHEN KÖNIGSINSCHRIFTEN ALS 'PRIMÄRQUELLE'

Rainer Albertz

Von der Schwierigkeit einer historischen Rekonstruktion der Exilszeit

Die Exilszeit stellt in der biblischen Geschichtsdarstellung ein finsteres Loch dar.[1] Etwas Licht fällt nur auf die Ränder, wie es zum Exil kam (2. Kön. 24–25; Jer. 39; 52; 2. Chr. 36) und wie es endete (Esr. 1–6) und auf einige Einzelereignisse, so das Scheitern der Gedalja-Herrschaft und dessen Folgen noch ganz am Anfang der Exilszeit (Jer. 40.1–43.7; 2. Kön. 25.22-26) und die Begnadigung Jajochins durch Awil-Marduk etwa in dessen Mitte (562 v. Chr.). Allein in 2. Chr. 36 wird der Versuch unternommen, das gähnende Loch dieser Epoche zu überbrücken. Doch mehr als zwei Verse vermag auch diese biblische Geschichtsdarstellung über die Exilszeit nicht zu sagen (20-21). An konkreten Ereignissen weiß sie nur zu berichten, daß die von Nebukadnezar Deportierten 'bis zur Errichtung des persischen Königreiches seiner und seiner Söhne Knechte wurden' und ihr Heimatland 70 Jahre 'der Verwüstung ruhte'. Ansonsten füllt sie die Lücke mit einer Reihe von theologischen Deutungen. Der Geschichtsverlauf erstarrt wortwörtlich zur 'Sabbatruhe' des Landes.

Dieser Quellenbefund im Alten Testament stellt jede historische Rekonstruktion der Exilszeit vor große Schwierigkeiten. Diejenigen Forscher, die nach wie vor bereit sind, den biblischen Texten nach sorgfältiger literarturgeschichtlicher Analyse und klarer Tendenzkritik einen mehr oder minder großen Quellenwert neben den außerbiblischen

---

1. Die folgenden Ausführungen stehen im Zusammenhang des Bandes 'Exilzeit', den ich für die Biblische Enzyklopädie schreibe.

Quellen zur Rekonstruktion der Geschichte Israels einzuräumen, nennen wir sie die Maximalisten, stehen für diese Epoche mit ziemlich leeren Händen da; da sie kaum biblische Quellen haben, wandeln sie sich notgedrungen zu Minimalisten. Aber auch diejenigen Forscher, die den biblischen Texten wegen ihrer späten Entstehung und ihres verzerrenden theologischen Interesses die historische Glaubwürdigkeit mehr oder minder radikal absprechen und statt dessen den außerbiblischen archäologischen, ikonographischen und textlichen Quellen als 'Primärquellen' den Vorzug bei der Rekonstruktion der Geschichte Israels einräumen wollen, nennen wir sie die Minimalisten, stehen vor dem Ernstfall für ihren methodischen Ansatz: Sie können anhand der Exilszeit testen, ob eine Rekonstruktion der Geschichte allein aus außerbiblischen Quellen, wo sie mangels Masse nicht doch heimlich auf die biblische Geschichtsdarstellung schielen können, überhaupt möglich ist.

Machen wir die Probe aufs Exempel! In keiner zeitgenössischen außerbiblischen Quelle aus dem 6. Jh. ist die Exilierung eines wie groß auch immer zu bestimmenden Anteils der judäischen Bevölkerung nach Babylonien erwähnt. Von der Belagerung und Einnahme der 'Stadt Judas' (*URU Ja-a-ḫu-du*), worunter wohl Jerusalem zu verstehen ist, durch Nebukadnezar am 2. Adar seines 7. Regierungsjahrs (16. März 597 v. Chr.) erfahren wir aus der babylonischen Chronik (Grayson 1975a: 102; Nr. 5, rev. Z. 11-13). Diese Quelle ist nicht zeitgenössisch, sondern stammt frühestens aus der persischen, vielleicht sogar erst aus der seleukidischen Zeit, d.h. ist jünger als das Deuteronomistische Geschichtswerk in der üblichen Datierung. Sofern man ihr trotz ihres jungen Alters wegen ihrer erkennbaren gelehrten Akribie historische Glaubwürdigkeit zugesteht, belegt sie die Gefangennahme des regierenden Königs (Jojachin), und die Einnahme eines schweren Tributs (*bilassa kabittu*). Der Begriff kann eine Deportation mit umfassen, muß es aber nicht. Die Zerstörung und Brandschatzung der Stadt durch die Babylonier (587/86), die jetzt archäologisch durch die Grabung Y. Shilos am Südosthügel bezeugt ist (*NEAE*, 709), kommt bekanntlich in der babylonischen Chronik Nr.5 nicht vor, da diese mit dem 11. Regierungsjahr Nebukadnezars (594) abbricht (vgl. Grayson 1975a: 102).

Die einzige außerbiblische Quelle, die von einer Ansiedlung jüdischer Gefangener neben phönizischen, syrischen und ägyptischen 'in den am besten geeigneten Teilen von Babylonien' berichtet, ist die Babylonaica des Berossus (c. Ap. I, 137-38, vgl. Burstein 1978: 27).

Auch sie stammt erst aus hellenistischer Zeit und ist zudem nur auszug-
sweise und sekundär bei Josephus überliefert. Da diese Deportation
nach der Darstellung des Berossos direkt im Anschluß an die Schlacht
von Karkemisch im Jahr 605 stattgefunden haben müßte, noch bevor
Nebukadnezar nach der babylonischen Chronik überhaupt in südlichere
Gefilde vorstieß (Z. 15-20), ist diese Nachricht historisch unglaub-
würdig. Es kann sich entweder nur um eine begrenzte Zahl jüdischer
Söldner im ägyptischen Heer gehandelt haben; oder aber Berossos hat
spätere, ihm bekannte Deportationen summarisch schon in das Akzes-
sionsjahr Nebukadnezars verlegt.

Auch sonst ist die außerbiblische Evidenz für das babylonische Exil
eher kläglich: aus den sog. Weidner-Tafeln ist belegt, daß 'Jojachin,
der König von Juda', seine 5 Söhne und weitere 5 namentlich genannte
und 8 unbenannte Judäer am Hofe Nebukadnezars Ölrationen bezogen.
Eine dieser Rationen wurde im Jahr 592 ausgegeben (Weidner 1939:
924-31; Tafel C); das Datum der anderen ist unbekannt; das Archiv
insgesamt soll Texte aus den Jahren 595–570 umfassen. Dies belegt die
Exilierung Jojachins und einiger weniger Leute aus seiner Familie und
seinem Hofstaat. Aus den vielen neubabylonischen Wirtschafts-
urkunden des 6. Jh. hat R. Zadok dagegen nur etwa eine Handvoll
Personen als Judäer aufgrund ihres Namens identifizieren können
(1979: 38-40; 1984: 294-97). Erst im Murashû-Archiv aus der 2. Hälfte
des 5. Jh. wird der Anteil jüdischer Namen erwähnenswert (2, 8
prozent). Aufgrund dieses mageren außerbiblischen Befundes würde
niemand auf die Idee kommen, eine nennenswerte Deportation von
Judäern in babylonischer Zeit anzunehmen.

Wenn es nach den außerbiblischen Texten eine Exilierung Judas
gegeben hat, dann geschah diese 701 durch Sanherib, der sich im Tay-
lor-Zylinder rühmt, 200150 Menschen und Tiere deportiert zu haben.[2]
Auch das berühmte Niniveh-Relief 'Die Eroberung von Lachish'
(*ANEP*, 129-32) bildet eine Gruppe judäischer Deportierter ab. Selbst
wenn man die hohe Zahl anzweifeln mag—der Assyriologe W. Mayer

---

2.   *TUAT* 1.4, 389, Z. 24-27; wenn Sanherib Z. 27 berichtet, er habe die Menschen und Tiere aus den eroberten judäischen Städten 'herausgeführt' (*waṣû Š*) und
'der Beute zugerechnet' (*šallatiš manû*), dann ist damit der Abtransport impliziert.
Das Wort *šallatu* hat den semantischen Gehalt des 'Weggeführten' (vgl. das Verb
šalālu 'fortführen, plündern' und *AHw*, 1142; 1148). Es besteht darum kein Anlaß
aufgrund der Formulierung, die mehrfach in ähnlichem Zusammenhang vorkommt,
eine Deportation Sanheribs zu bezweifeln.

rechnet aber immer noch mit etwa 100.000 Menschen (1995: 41-45) —nach dieser Quellenlage müßte man die wirkliche Exilierung Judas 100 Jahre früher datieren und die biblische Periodisierung 'Exilszeit' für das 6. Jh.—sei es nun 597/587 bis 539 oder 520—grundsätzlich in Frage stellen.

Nimmt man zu diesen textlichen und bildlichen außerbiblischen Quellen die archäologischen Befunde in Juda hinzu, so ergibt sich ebenfalls ein undeutliches Bild. Während man früher die Zerstörung judäischer Städte gerne pauschal mit der in der Bibel erwähnten Eroberung Jerusalems 587/86 durch Nebukadnezar in Zusammenhang brachte und etwa W.F. Albright daraus eine weitgehende Entvölkerung des Landes folgerte, die fast dem chronistischen Bild von 2. Chr. 36.21 entsprach, sieht das Bild nach heutiger Einschätzung differenzierter aus.[3] Die Städte Lachish, Tell Bet-Mirsim, Bet-Shemesh, Beersheba und die Festung Arad wurden schon 701 zerstört und nur zum Teil (Lachish, Beersheba, Arad), und dann verkleinert, wieder aufgebaut. Die Zerstörung von En-Gedi fand erst später (582?) statt; ob Bet-Zur zerstört wurde, ist nach neueren Erkenntnissen fraglich; sicher ist, daß die Städte des benjaminitischen Nordens nur partiell zerstört wurden wie Tell el-Ful, oder ganz der Zerstörung entgingen wie Tell en-Naṣbe (Mizpa), Gibeon und Bethel. Mehr oder minder sicher mit den Babyloniern können Zerstörungen von Jerusalem, Ramat-Rahel, Lachish, Gezer, Tell el-Ḥesi, Arad und Tell Mshash[4] in Verbindung gebracht werden. Eigenartigerweise wird von archäologischer Seite bisher nicht versucht, den Bevölkerungsverlust, den Juda durch die assyrischen bzw. babylonischen Eroberungen und Deportationen erlitten hat, genauer abzuschätzen. Ich kenne zur Zeit nur die Kalkulation, die A. Ofer aufgrund des Israel-Surveys vorgetragen hat (vgl. *NEAE*, 816). Er kommt für das judäische Bergland zu einem Rückgang der Siedlungsfläche und damit der Bevölkerungszahl um etwa 25 prozent vom 8. Jh. zum 7./6. Jh. Allerdings betrifft diese Berechnung nur einen Teil des judäischen Staates, unberücksichtigt bleibt in ihr die Shefela, die

---

3.   Vgl. dazu die entsprechenden Artikel von *NEAE*. Meine Einschätzung stimmt weitgehend mit Barstad 1996: 47-76 überein; nur ordnet er noch die Zerstörungen von Bet Mirsim und Bet-Shemesh den Kriegszügen Nebukadnezars zu (47).

4.   Auch wenn die Zerstörung der letzten drei genannten Orte im Süden wahrscheinlich auf das Konto der Edomiter geht, so standen deren Angriffe doch im Zusammenhang der babylonischen Strafaktionen gegen Juda, vgl. 2. Kön 24.1-2.

Hauptstadt Jerusalem samt ihrem Umland und das benjaminitische Gebiet. Auch wird nicht zwischen dem Bevölkerungsverlust, der aufgrund der assyrischen Deportation Sanheribs (701) anzunehmen ist, und den späteren babylonischen Exilierungen differenziert. Es hat den Anschein, als sei auch für die Archäologie Palästinas die Exilszeit ohne deutliche Befunde und damit ohne Interesse. Oder ist dieser Eindruck falsch? Falls mich jemand eines Besseren belehren könnte, wäre ich ihm dankbar.

Ob ein nennenswertes babylonisches Exil überhaupt stattfand, ist also nach den außerbiblischen Quellen eher fraglich. Auch die Geschichte Judas läßt sich im 6. Jh. aus außerbiblischen Quellen nicht aufhellen. So bleibt diese Epoche ein finsteres Loch. Die Maximalisten, die dieses Loch aus den biblischen Geschichtsberichten auch nicht viel aufzuhellen vermögen, können immerhin aus der prophetischen Literatur und der Theologiegeschichte des 6. und 5. Jahrhunderts aufweisen, welche Erschütterungen das Babylonische Exil auslöste und zu welchen Neuansätzen es trieb.[5] Seltsam ist jedoch, daß auch viele der Minimalisten entscheidende Wandlungen der Religions- und Theologiegeschichte Israels in eben diese historisch kaum faßbare Epoche setzten. Die Exilszeit wird dabei nicht selten, so lautet mein Vorwurf, als eine *black box* benutzt, in die alles das, dessen Historizität man in der vorexilischen Epoche Israels anzweifelt, unkontrolliert hineingeschoben wird. Wie kann aber das, was nach den Kriterien der Minimalisten historisch kaum von Bedeutung gewesen ist, literatur-, religions- und theologiegeschichtlich derartige Wirkungen gezeitigt haben?

Die neubabylonischen Königsinschriften als 'Primärquelle'

Die Entgegensetzung von späten, tendenziösen und darum historisch wertlosen biblischen 'Sekundärquellen' und zeitgenössischen und darum historisch zuverlässigen außerbiblischen 'Primärquellen' krankt daran, daß man sich aufgrund der besonderen Fundlage in Palästina häufig falsche Vorstellungen über letztere macht. In Palästina sind —aufgrund der Vergänglichkeit des Schreibmaterials (Papyrus) und der vielen Turbulenzen in seiner Geschichte—aus dem 1. JT. v. Chr. kaum literarische Texte erhalten geblieben. Darum fehlen aus dem Siedlungsgebiet des alten Israel und Juda z.B. all' die Gattungen, die wir etwa aus Mesopotamien, Syrien und Ägypten zur Genüge kennen:

5.	Vgl. etwa Albertz 1996–97: 375-459.

Königsinschriften, Hymnen, Gebete, Kultrituale, Omen-Serien, Epen, Spruchsammlungen und Weisheitsdichtungen. Gefunden wurden bisher fast nur kurze Gebrauchstexte, die auf Tonscherben geschrieben oder in Stein oder Metall eingeritzt worden sind, Inschriften, Briefe und Notizen, überwiegend aus der wirtschaftlichen oder militärischen Verwaltung. Auch die Archäologie Palästinas hat meist Profanbauten, Tore, Lagerhäuser, Paläste und Wohnhäuser, aber nur ganz wenige eisenzeitliche Heiligtümer aus Israel und Juda ans Licht gebracht (Arad, Dan, 'Bull-Site' u.a.). Daraus hat sich unter Alttestamentlern —so scheint mir—das Vorurteil in den Köpfen festgesetzt, im Unterschied zu den theologisch aufgeladenen Bibeltexten seien die außerbiblischen 'Primärquellen' viel profaner, weniger tendenziös und darum historisch glaubwürdiger. Das ist aber ein falscher Eindruck, der nur mit der Gattungsdifferenz der Texte zusammenhängt. Schon die wenigen literarischen Texte, die wir im 1. JT. aus der näheren Umwelt Israels haben, wie die Mesha-Stele, die—immer noch schwer deutbaren —Inschriften von Deir Allā oder die Achikar-Sprüche, sprechen schon eine sehr viel explizitere religiöse Sprache. Auch die neu gefundene Inschrift aus Dan, deren erhaltene Teile die Ansprüche des aramäischen Königs zwar nicht theologisch untermauern, ist, wenn die Rekonstruktion von I. Kottsieper richtig ist, daß Hasael für sich die Tötung Jorams und Ahasjas in Anspruch nimmt,[6] die nach 2. Kön. 9 Jehu vollzogen hat, nicht weniger tendenziös als die biblische Erzählung.

Wie stark die Gattung der Königsinschriften von einer theologisch begründeten politischen Tendenz beherrscht wird, wird vollends deutlich, wenn man die neubabylonischen Königsinschriften betrachtet, die in großer Zahl gefunden worden sind.

Die Inschriften Nebukadnezars, Neriglissars und Nabonids sind alle zeitgenössische Quellen des 6. Jh., das heißt für die israelitische Exilszeit; und dies um so mehr als Juda nicht nur unter die Herrschaft der neubabylonischen Könige kam, sondern ein Teil seiner Bevölkerung ins babylonische Kernland deportiert und dort angesiedelt wurde. Eine Gruppe von Exilierten um den gefangenen König Jojachin befand sich sogar unmittelbar in der Residenz. Allerdings sind die Königsinschriften keine Primärquellen für die Geschichte Judas oder der babylonischen Gola. Diese haben schon deswegen nur geringe Chancen, in den neubabylonischen Königsinschriften Erwähnung zu finden, weil

---

6. Sein Artikel erscheint demnächst in AOAT, 250 (I. Kottsieper; Münster: Ugarit Verlag, 1998).

sich die neubabylonischen Könige, anders als ihre assyrischen Vorgänger kaum ihrer militärisch-außenpolitischen, sondern fast ausschlie-
ßlich ihrer kultisch-innenpolitischen Großtaten rühmen, die sie in
Tempelrenovierungen, mit reichen Weihgaben an die Tempel, und
durch prächtigen Ausbau der Städte Babyloniens unter Beweis gestellt
haben. Und wo der außenpolitisch-militärische Bereich einmal mehr in
den Blick kommt, wie etwa beim Bau und der Einweihung des neuen
Palastes Nebukadnezars,[7] waren Juda und die Judäer nicht bedeutend
genug, um erwähnt zu werden, bzw. ist ihre Erwähnung durch Textab-
bruch verloren gegangen. Der 'Hof- und Staatskalender Nebukadnezars' (vgl. Unger 1970: 282-94), der im erhaltenen Text als Teil-
nehmer der Einweihungsfeierlichkeiten nach den babylonischen Wür-
denträgern immerhin die Könige der unterworfenen Städte Tyrus,
Gaza, Sidon, Arwad und Ashdod nennt (V, 23-27), könnte durchaus
einmal auch Jojachin erwähnt haben.

Die Königsinschriften sind aber sehr wohl eine 'zeitgenössische
Primärqelle' für das religiös-politische Klima des neubabylonischen
Reichs, in dem die Judäer der Exilzeit lebten. Und deswegen sind sie
eine Quelle für die tendenziöse Geschichtstheologie dieser Epoche, die
den biblischen Texten aus derselben Zeit (z.B. Deuteronomistisches
Geschichtswerk, Deuterojesaja) gar nicht so fern stehen. Ich möchte
das anhand einer Inschrift des letzten neubabylonischen Königs,
Nabonid, der 556-539 v. Chr. regierte, erläutern.

Der Gründungsmythos des neubabylonischen Reiches
Auf der leider nicht ganz vollständig erhaltenen, aus Babylon stam-
menden Basaltstele in Istanbul,[8] die wahrscheinlich aus den ersten
Jahren seiner Regierung stammt, reflektiert Nabonid darüber, warum
ausgerechnet er, 'in dessen Herz das Königtum nicht vorhanden war'
(VII, 45-52), den babylonischen Königsthron bestiegen habe. Er führt
dabei seine Thronbesteigung, die realgeschichtlich eine Usurpation war,
nicht nur auf den göttlichen Befehl Marduks zurück (V, 8-10), sondern
ordnet sie zudem in einen großen geschichtstheologischen Horizont
ein, der die ganze Geschichte des neubabylonischen Reiches umfaßt.

---

7.   Vgl. Langdon und Zehnpfund 1912: 94-95; 114-15; 134-37; Nbk 9, III, 27-
59 ; Nbk 14, II, 1-9; Nbk 15, VII, 34-52.
8.   Langdon und Zehnpfund 1912: 270-89, Nbd 8; vgl. *ANET*, 308-11. Die
Nabonid-Inschriften hat H. Schaudig in seiner gerade abgeschlossenen Münsteraner
Dissertation neu bearbeitet.

Eigenartigerweise beginnt Nabonid diesen Rückblick lange vor der Gründung des Reiches durch Nabopolassar, der ab 626 als Scheich des Meerlandes den Kampf mit den assyrischen Besatzern aufnahm. Kolumne I berichtet von einem assyrischen König, der 'Böses sann', die Bevölkerung Babyloniens erbarmungslos auszulöschen trachtete, die Heiligtümer Babylons verwüstete, seine Kulte ruinierte und den Gott Marduk nach Assur verschleppte (I, 1-17). Gemeint ist Sanherib, der nach mehreren babylonischen Aufständen 689 Babylon eroberte und nicht einmal vor der Zerstörung des Marduktempels Esangila zurückschreckte, seine Kultstatue raubte und die Stadt durch die Euphratwasser flutete, so daß sie für ein Jahrzehnt unbewohnbar blieb.

Es geht aber Nabonid nicht um dieses traumatische politische Ereignis als solches. Sanherib konnte sich vielmehr nur so blasphemisch an Babylon vergehen, weil Marduk damals seinem Land zürnte. So heißt es zusammenfassend nach den Untaten des assyrischen Königs: 'Nach dem Zorn Gottes tat er dem Lande' (I, 18-19). Und in dieser theologischen Perspektive wird die Zerstörung Babylons Ausgangspunkt einer langen Kette von Ereignissen, die zur Gründung des neubabylonischen Reiches und darüber hinaus führt.

21 Jahre dauerte der Zorn Marduks während des Exils seiner Statue in Assur, bis Shamash-shuma-ukin im Jahr 668, nachdem schon sein Vater Asarhaddon den Wiederaufbau Babylons begonnen hatte, die— bzw. eine neue—Mardukstatue zurückbrachte (I, 20-25). Dann beruhigte sich sein Zorn und er gedachte wieder seiner Stadt und seines Tempels (Z. 26-34). Diese erneute Zuwendung Marduks wirkte sich nun als ein Strafgericht über die Assyrer aus. Es war schon in der Ermordung Sanheribs 681 zum Zuge gekommen (Z. 35-41); dessen Rolle, als Werkzeug des göttlichen Zornes fungiert zu haben, rechtfertigte also keineswegs seine abscheuliche Untat. Zu seinem Ziel kam es aber erst, als Marduk dem Begründer des neubabylonischen Reiches, Nabopolasser, bei seinem Befreiungskampf gegen die Assyrer ab 614 den König der Meder als Bündnisgenossen zuführte und mit dessen Hilfe wie eine Sintflut ganz Assyrien niederwalzte (II, 1-10). Wenn nun die Kriege der vereinigten Babylonier und Meder gegen die Assyrer von 614–605 als Vergeltung (*gimillu*) und Rache (*tuktû*) bezeichnet werden, die Marduk für Babylon übte (*târu*, bzw. *riābu*), dann bringt Nabonid den Untergang des neuassyrischen und den Aufstieg des neubabylonischen Reiches unmittelbar mit der Zerstörung Babylons durch Sanheribs rund 80 Jahre zuvor in Verbindung. Aus der tiefsten

Erniedrigung Babylons war durch Marduks Vergeltung der größte Triumph der Stadt geworden.

Daß es sich hierbei um einen regelrechten Gründungsmythos des neubabylonischen Reiches handelt (so Beaulieu 1989: 115), auf den Nabonid Bezug nimmt, macht ein literarischer Text deutlich, den P. Gerardi unter dem Titel 'Declaring War in Mesopotamia' veröffentlicht hat (1986: 34-37) und der wahrscheinlich aus der Regierungszeit Nabopolassars stammt. Hier wirft der babylonische dem assyrischen König vor, zum Feind Babyloniens geworden zu sein, seinen Reichtum geplündert und das Eigentum Esangilas und der Hauptstadt zur Schau gestellt und—wahrscheinlich nach Ninive—abtransportiert zu haben. Mit letzterem ist wahrscheinlich wieder das Sakrileg Sanheribs gemeint, auf den und dessen Eroberung Babylons später im Text ausdrücklich Bezug genommen wird (rev. Z. 7-8). Darum, so fährt Nabopolassar fort, habe Marduk ihn aus dem Seeland zur Herrschaft über Land und Leute ausersehen, um 'Vergeltung für das Land Akkad zu üben' (obv. Z. 12: *ana turru gimil māt URI.KI*). Und so werde er in Eroberung und Zerstörung Ninives die 'Vergeltung für Babylon vollziehen' (rev. Z. 3: *gimil utarri ana TIN.TIR.KI*). Egal ob man diesen Text noch vor oder erst nach der Eroberung Ninives (612) ansetzt, er bezeugt in jedem Fall, daß schon die Feldzüge der vereinigten Babylonier und Meder gegen die Assyrer, die in die Errichtung des neubabylonischen Reiches einmündeten, unter Berufung auf 'Marduks Rache für Babylon' geführt und gerechtfertigt worden sind. Wenn in Zeile III, 21 des sog. 'Nabopolassar Epic' (Grayson 1975b: 82-85) '[Übe] Vergeltung für das Land Akkad' (*[x (x)] x gimil URI.KI EN [...]*) zu ergänzen ist, dann gehörte der Topos sogar zum neubabylonischen Krönungsritual. Nabonid griff in seiner Stele somit auf den Gründungsmythos des neubabylonischen Reiches zürück, der seit dem Reichsgründer das Selbstverständnis dieses Reichs ganz wesentlich bestimmt hatte. Über diesen theologischen Gründungsmythos bekamen geschichtliche Ereignisse, die 60 bzw. 135 Jahre vergangen waren, für ihn unmittelbare Bedeutung für seine Gegenwart und Zukunft.

Nabonids Regierungserklärung im Rahmen des Gründungsmythos
Es ist nun interessant zu sehen, wie Nabonid seine neue Politik, die er beabsichtigt, in den babylonischen Gründungsmythos einzeichnet, jene von ihm her begründet und diesen damit neu akzentuiert.

Nabonid erwähnt in seiner Stele, wie der König der Meder alle Heiligtümer Assyriens verwüstete, ganz so wie es Sanherib mit Babylon getan hatte (vgl. II, 14-19 mit I, 8-13). Das blieb noch im Rahmen der Vergeltung Marduks und war damit theologisch gerechtfertigt. Aber der Mederkönig war darüber hinausgegangen, er hatte auch die Tempel der Städte an der Grenze Babyloniens total verwüstet, die sich nicht mit dem babylonischen König verbündet hatten (II, 20-31). Unter diesen waren auch die Stadt Harran und ihr Sin-Tempel Eḫulḫul gewesen, die 610 v. Chr. von den Medern und Babyloniern zerstört worden waren, nachdem sich die Assyrer dahin zurückgezogen hatten (vgl. X, 12-15). Damit war aber für Nabonid, dessen Mutter Adad-guppi/ḫappe sehr wahrscheinlich aus Harran stammte und am babylonischen Hof aufsteigen konnte, bei der Gründung des neubabylonischen Reiches ein Unrecht geschehen, das dieses belastete und auf Wiedergutmachung drängte.

Nabonid versucht in seiner Darstellung, den Reichsgründer Nabopolassar vom Sakrileg dieser Tempelzerstörungen zu entlasten, indem er diese allein dem wilden Mederhaufen in die Schuhe schiebt und behauptet, daß jener 'nicht seine Hand an die Kulte aller Götter legte', sondern tief darüber trauerte (II, 31-41). Allerdings kann auch er nicht umhin zuzugeben, daß sich die Kultbilder des Sin aus Harran jetzt im Marduk-Tempel von Babylon befanden (X, 32-51); doch stellt Nabonid dies als reine Schutzmaßnahme dar.

Nach dem nun folgenden Geschichtsrückblick haben seine Vorgänger, die neubabylonischen Könige Nebukadnezar (? III) und Neriglissar (IV) die Unordnung, die die Assyrer in die Kult- und Götterwelt gebracht hatten, durch die Wiederherstellung und prächtige Ausstattung von Tempeln und Kultriten in Babylonien wieder beseitigt. Auch er selber hatte, nachdem er anstelle des ungeeigneten, 'gleichsam gegen den Willen der Götter' (IV, 40) regierenden Labashi-Marduk von Marduk 'zur Herrschaft über das Land erhoben worden' (V, 8-10) und von Nebukadnezar im Traum bestätigt worden war (VI), die reichliche Versorgung babylonischer Tempel fortgesetzt (VIII–IX). Nun aber, nachdem die Ansprüche der Götter im babylonischen Kernland weitgehend befriedigt waren, war es nach Nabonids Darstellung nur konsequent, nun auch die bei der Niederwerfung der Assyrer zerstörten Tempel in den Randregionen mit in die königliche Kultversorgung einzubeziehen.

Marduk, so stellt es Nabonid dar, hatte auf ihn regelrecht gewartet, um ihn mit der Rückführung und Versöhnung der immer noch verschleppten und darum zürnenden Götter zu beauftragen. Nach 54 Jahren, die Sin im babylonischen Exil verbracht hatte, sah Nabonid den Zeitpunkt der Versöhnung gekommen und die Rückkehr Sins nach Harran durch Marduks ausdrücklichen Befehl angeordnet (IX, 12-31). Der Wiederaufbau des Sin-Tempels in Harran war somit für Nabonid das Gebot der Stunde, dem er zu folgen beabsichtigte.

Nabonid geht es hier, noch ganz am Anfang seiner Regierung, darum, die Kontinuität seiner Politik mit seinen tatkräftigen Vorgängern zu betonen. Er bezieht sich darum auf den Gründungs-mythos des Reiches und bleibt auch noch ganz im Rahmen der Marduktheologie. Dennoch ist die Umorientierung von Reichspolitik und Reichstheologie, die er hier beabsichtigt und die er später trotz aller Schwierigkeiten[9] und Widerstände (s.u.) konsequent betreiben sollte, erheblich. Man unterschätzt diese bei weitem, wollte man den Tempelbau in Harran nur als Ausdruck einer persönlichen Glaubenspräferenz oder sentimentalen Wiedergutmachung für die Heimat seiner Mutter ansehen. Was Nabonid mit der Einbeziehung Harrans in die Wiederaufbau- und Versorgungspflicht des babylonischen Königs bezwecken wollte, wird erst sichtbar, wenn man die Reichs- und Kultpolitik seiner Vorgänger zum Vergleich heranzieht. Ich kann dies hier nur andeuten:

Nebukadnezar war es darum gegangen, die rivalisierenden Städte Babyloniens und das ganze Reich durch ein einziges repräsentatives lokales Zentrum zu einen; deswegen baute er unermüdlich seine 'Lieblingsstadt' Babylon zur prachtvollen Metropole aus. Es ist kein Zufall, daß er dabei etwa seinen neuen Süd-Palast, den er unter Aufbietung der Wirtschafts- und Arbeitskraft seines Riesenreiches in kürzester Zeit prachtvoll hochzog, 'Einigungsband des Landes' (Langdon und Zehnpfund 1912: 114-15; 136-37) und 'Einigungsband der großen Völker' (Langdon und Zehnpfund 1912: 94-95) nannte. Die Reichspolitik Nebukadnezars hatte somit darin bestanden, die gesamte Wirtschaftskraft des Reiches, die Gewinne der Kriegszüge, die Tribute der Provinzen und die Arbeitskraft der Deportierten einseitig zur Förderung des babylonischen Kernlandes zu nutzen, während die anderen Teile

---

9.   Harran lag noch im medischen Einflußbereich und gelangte erst ab dem Aufstand des Kyros gegen die Meder (553 v. Chr.) unter babylonische Herrschaft, vgl. Nabonids spätere Rechtfertigung der Verzögerung des Tempelbaus in Langdon und Zehnpfund 1912: 218-21; *TUAT*, 2.4, 494-95.

des Reiches leer ausgingen. Der Gründungsmythos 'Marduks Rache für Babylon' führte somit innenpolitisch zu einer Einbahnstraße, zu einer Ausblutung der Provinzen zugunsten der Zentrale. Begleitet wurde diese zentralistische Wirtschaftspolitik mit der religionspolitischen Anstrengung, Marduk nicht nur zum höchsten Gott Babyloniens zu erheben, sondern ihn auch als Reichsgott zu etablieren. Dazu war dieser aber als traditioneller Stadtgott von Babylon, der im Gründungsmythos auch noch so stark zugunsten seiner Stadt, bzw. des babylonischen Kernlandes Stellung bezogen hatte, wenig geeignet.

Der Wiederaufbau des Sin-Tempels von Harran, den Nabonid propagierte, bedeutete demgegenüber nicht weniger, als daß erstmals in der Geschichte des neubabylonischen Reiches die Wirtschaftskraft des Reiches und der Zentrale zugunsten einer Provinzregion umgeleitet werden sollte. Welchen Bruch ein solches Vorhaben mit der traditionellen Kult- und Reichspolitik darstellte, zeigt der geballte Widerstand, der Nabonid aus der Hauptstadt und allen wichtigen babylonischen Städte entgegenschlug, den Nabonid später in seiner Harran-Inschrift als Aufstand gegen den Gott Sin beschreibt, der den Gott veranlaßt habe, ihn aus Babylon in die arabische Wüste zu entfernen (Röllig 1964: I, 14-20).

Mir scheint, daß Nabonid ein polyzentrischer Aufbau des Reiches vorschwebte; auch der immer noch mysteriöse zehnjährige Aufenthalt in Tema ließe sich in eine solche Konzeption gut einordnen. Immerhin weilte Nabonid hier—entgegen späterer Legendenbildung—keineswegs als Kranker[10] oder Wahnsinniger,[11] sondern hat diese auch wirtschaftlich interessante arabische Oasenstadt zu einer regelrechten Residenz mit vorzüglichen Nachrichtenverbindungen zur alten Hauptstadt ausgebaut. Mit dieser Dezentralisierung verbunden war der immer entschlossenere Versuch Nabonids, den Mondgott Sin, der weniger lokal festgelegt war als Marduk, sondern sowohl im babylonischen Kernland (Ur) als auch im Norden, Westen (Harran) und Süden des Reiches (Arabien) verehrt wurde, anstelle Marduks als Reichsgott zu etablieren. Dies rief den erbitterten Widerstand der babylonischen Aristokratie, insbesondere der Mardukpriesterschaft hervor, an dem Nabonid scheiterte. Wenn man sieht, wie sich Nabonid in seiner Spätzeit nicht mehr nur 'König von Babylon' nannte, sondern auch 'König der Welt' oder 'König der vier Weltgegenden' (Langdon und Zehnpfund 1912: 218-

10. So 4QOrNab.
11. So die in Dan. 4 auf Nebukadnezar übertragene Tradition.

19) wie die assyrischen Könige, wenn man weiter sieht, wie er in seiner Harran-Stele die 'Leute von Akkad und Hatti' (Röllig 1964: II, 8; III, 19), d.h. Babylonien und Syrien-Palästina, auf eine Stufe stellte, dann wird erkennbar, wie weit er schließlich den Gründungsmythos des neubabylonischen Reiches hinter sich gelassen hatte. Doch erst den Persern war es vergönnt, eine stärker dezentrale Reichsstruktur politisch durchzusetzen und sowohl theologisch als auch kultpolitisch abzustützen.

Methodische Folgerungen

Zum Abschluß möchte ich einige methodische Gesichtspunkte herausstellen, die sich aus den neubabylonischen Königsinschriften für eine Rekonstruktion der babylonischen Geschichte des 6. Jh. ergeben, die aber—so meine ich—auch Gesichtspunkte für den Umgang mit biblischen Texten dieser Zeit und darüber hinaus abgeben können:

Die neubabylonischen Königsinschriften sind den historischen Ereignissen, von denen sie berichten, so nahe, daß sie als zeitgenössische Primärquellen für die politische Geschichte des neubabylonischen Reiches zu betrachten sind.

Dennoch schildern sie die historischen Ereignisse nicht in der bei uns üblich gewordenen rein innerweltlichen Perspektive. Es handelt sich vielmehr—in den Inschriften Nabonids noch expliziter als in denen der anderen neubabylonischen Könige—um eine stark theologisch durchtränkte Geschichtsschreibung, nach der, trotz aller Aktivitäten der Könige, letztlich das Handeln der Götter den Geschichtsverlauf bestimmt. Sie zürnen und erbarmen sich ihrer Stadt, sie rächen das ihr angetane Unrecht. Sie erwählen und beauftragen die Könige, sie bestimmen die Zeitpunkte für ihre Handlungen. Erfolgreiches königliches Handeln kann es nur in der Übereinstimmung mit göttlichem Handeln geben, die Könige sind Werkzeuge der Götter. Doch königliche Untaten können, wie das Beispiel Sanheribs zeigt, zwar göttlichen Zorn realisieren, werden aber deswegen nicht entschuldigt, sondern später von den Göttern bestraft.

Mit der theologischen Sicht der Geschichte geht eine Verknüpfung geschichtlicher Ereignisse über lange Zeiträume einher, wie der Gründungsmythos des neubabylonischen Reiches zeigt, der auf die Zerstörung Babylons ca. 80 Jahre vor der Reichsgründung Bezug nimmt; die behandelte Inschrift Nabonids läßt sogar ca. 135 Jahre Revue passieren. Die Einzelereignisse erhalten durch diese theologische

Verknüpfung einen bestimmten Sinn, eindeutige Wertungen und eine klare Tendenz.[12] Aus der Tendenz des Geschichtsverlaufes leitet Nabonid eine ganz bestimmte Option für die Zukunft ab. Es handelt sich somit explizit um paradigmatische Geschichtsschreibung.

Vieles erinnert hier an die Geschichtsschreibung des Deuternomistischen Geschichtswerkes,[13] an die Völkersprüche[14] und Deuterojesaja,[15] die alle aus der gleichen Epoche stammen. Man kann mit Fug und Recht sagen: Das 6. Jh. war unter neubabylonischer Ägide regelrecht von Geschichtstheologie geschwängert.

Moderner Tendenzkritik ist es ein leichtes, das leitende Interesse der Nabonid-Inschrift zu durchschauen. Der babylonische Gründungsmythos ist für sie die durchsichtige theologische Legitimation eines rücksichtslosen Hegemonialanspruchs der Jahrhunderte lang zu kurz gekommenen Babylonier. Das Interesse Nabonids am Tempelbau von Harran ist für sie nicht Ergebnis, sondern Ausgangspunkt der ganzen theologischen Geschichtskonstruktion, die kultische Maßnahme dabei nur fromme Verkleidung des Wunsches nach politischer und wirtschaftlicher und Umstrukturierung seines Reiches.

Eine solche historisch-kritische Durchleuchtung der neubabylonischen Königsinschriften einschließlich einer harten Tendenzkritik ist ein wichtiger und nötiger Schritt, um uns nachaufklärerischen Europäern einen Zugang des Verstehens zu diesen altorientalischen Inschriften zu ermöglichen. Dennoch wäre es falsch, unsere untheologische Geschichtssicht dabei absolut zu setzen und zum reduktionistischen Maßstab unserer Darstellung der Geschichte des neubabylonischen Reiches machen zu wollen. Insofern gelten für sie die gleichen methodischen Grundsätze wie für entsprechende biblische Texte, obgleich wir ihnen keinen normativen Anspruch an uns zubilligen.

Aber gerade weil die neubabylonischen Königsinschriften keinerlei normative Ansprüche erheben, deren Sicht zu destruieren, den Reiz eines emanzipatorischen Aktes haben könnte, können sie für den

12. Die Verbindung von 'events' zu einer 'narrative', die B. Becking aufgrund geschichtsphilosophischer Reflexionen als das Kennzeichnen der Historiographie herausstellt (s.o. 40-61), geschieht in den neubabylonischen Königsinschriften durch Aufdecken der theologischen Zusammenhänge.

13. Vgl. das Zürnen, Strafen und Erbarmen Gottes im Zusammenhang mit der Geschichte von Königen und Städten.

14. Vgl. z.B. die Vergeltung bzw. Rache JHWH, an Babylon in Jer. 51.6, 36, 56 und allgemein das Prinzip des gerechten Ausgleichs.

15. So die Periodisierung von Unheils- und Heilsperiode in Jes. 6.11; 40.1-2.

Alttestamentler—fern jeder Aufgeregtheit—vielleicht einige schlichte
Hinweise geben, wie mit einer solchen theologisierten antiken Geschichtsschreibung umzugehen sei:

Die Nabonid-Inschrift kann zum Beispiel zeigen, daß es falsch ist,
aus dem stark theologischen und tendenziösen Charakter einer
Geschichtsschreibung deren Unhistorizität zu folgern. Der theologische
Gründungsmythos des neubabylonischen Reiches, so gut sich damit die
totale Vernichtung assyrischer Städte und Tempel legitimieren ließ, ist
nicht erfunden. Die Zerstörung Babylons durch Sanherib 689 hat es
historisch gegeben; und sie ging auch nach unserer historischen Einschätzung über das Maß der im Vorderen Orient sonst vorkommenden
Verwüstungen hinaus. Normalerweise wurden bei einer Eroberung die
Tempel geschont, die Eroberer versuchten sich die Gunst ihrer Götter
zu sichern. Wenn Sanherib diese Regel mißachtete, dann ist das nur so
zu erklären, daß der Marduktempel zum Träger des anhaltenden anti-
assyrischen Widerstandes geworden war, aus dessen Schatz z.B. die
elamischen Verbündeten finanziert wurden. Dennoch war sein Vorge-
hen ein zum Himmel schreiendes Sakrileg. Das bedeutet: Selbst für die
Enstehung eines Gründungsmyhos ist es wahrscheinlicher, daß er aus
einer erregenden geschichtlichen Erfahrung erwachsen ist, als daß es
sich um eine reine Erfindung handelt.[16] Aber selbst wenn dies nicht
mehr mit Sicherheit zu klären wäre, kann nicht einfach mit dem Hin-
weis, es handele sich um einen Gründungsmythos, der pauschale Ver-
dacht der Unhistorizität erhoben werden. Es muß auch bei solchen stark
theologisch-tendenziösen Texten der methodische Grundsatz gelten,
daß im einzelnen durch kritische Nachfrage und—wenn möglich—
durch Vergleich mit anderen Quellen geklärt wird, welche Ereignisse
aus dem dargebotenen geschichtlich-theologischen Geflecht einen re-
algeschichtlichen Anhalt haben und wo etwa aus erkennbarem Interesse
der Ablauf geschönt oder erfunden wurde.[17] D.h. es bleibt gegenüber
einer solchen theologisch-tendenziösen Geschichtsschreibung überhaupt nichts anderes übrig, als die in letzter Zeit völlig zu Unrecht
geschmähte 'Substraktionsmethode' anzuwenden. Sie führt, wie oben

16. Insofern ist es eine weise Zurückhaltung, wenn K. van der Toorn, obwohl er
den Exodus als 'national charter myth' Israels bestimmt, dessen historischen Anhalt
nicht ganz leugnet (1996: 291-302). Zu meiner historischen Einschätzung des
Exodus vgl. Albertz 1995a: 185-87.

17. So etwa die Art, wie Nabonid die Rolle Nabopolassars bei der Zerstörung
des Harran-Tempels beschreibt.

an der Nabonid-Inschrift demonstriert, zu durchaus plausiblen histori-schen Ergebnissen.

Die theologischen Erklärungs- und Wertungsmuster der neubabyloni-schen Inschriften dürfen nun aber bei der historisch-kritischen Rekonstruktion auch nicht einfach als irrelevantes 'Beiwerk' wegge-strichen werden. Es läßt sich zeigen, daß der babylonische Grün-dungsmythos, obwohl nach unserer Sicht ein theologisches Konstrukt, dennoch die Politik des neubabylonischen Reiches real beeinflußt hat. Der Topos 'Marduks Rache für Babylon' hat nachweislich den Be-freiungskampf Nabopolassars gegen die Assyrer stark motiviert und damit zum Sieg der Babylonier und zur Legitimation ihrer Reichsgrün-dung beigetragen. Er hat auch noch die Außenpolitik Nebukadnezars erfolgreich geleitet, wenn dieser alles daransetzte, Ägypten, den letzten Verbündeten Assyriens, zu Lande[18] und zu Wasser[19] konsequent aus Syrien und Palästina fernzuhalten. Der gleiche Mythos hat jedoch nach Abschluß der Aufbauphase verhindert, von einer einseitigen Raubzugs-Politik zugunsten des babylonischen Kernlandes zu einer auf Ausgleich zwischen den Regionen des Reiches gerichteten Förder-Politik überzugehen. Nabonid hat das zwar noch im Anschluß an den Grün-dungsmythos versucht, doch er ist am Widerstand der durch ihn Pre-vilegierten gescheitert.

Schließlich würde man die Kultur- und Religionsgeschichte des neu-babylonischen Reiches völlig verzeichnen, wenn man die theologischen Dimensionen seiner Königsinschriften als irrelevant beiseite ließe. Es kommt vielmehr auch in unserer historischen Rekonstruktion darauf an herauszuarbeiten, warum sich etwa Nabonid in seinen Inschriften so und nicht anders präsentiert hat. D.h. die Geschichtssicht der neubaby-lonischen Könige bzw. ihrer Hoftheologen und unsere moderne Geschichtsauffassung müssen bei unserer historischen Rekonstruktion in einen Dialog miteinander treten. Innen- und Außenperspektive müssen sich bei einer Darstellung der Geschichte des neubabylonischen

---

18. Die Vertreibung Ägyptens aus Palästina war das eigentliche Kriegsziel des Feldzuges gegen das abtrünnige Jerusalem 587/6, das auch erreicht wurde. Während der 'Belagerungspause' wurde das ägyptische Heer so vernichtend geschlagen, daß Ägypten im 6. Jh. auf weitere Landoperationen nach Palästina verzichtete und seine Macht auf die Flotte verlegte, vgl. James 1991: 719.

19. Dies ist der Hintergrund der 13jährigen Belagerung von Tyros durch Nebukadnezar, die wahrscheinlich in die Jahre 585–572 eingeordnet werden muß, vgl. Katzenstein 1973: 328-30. Tyros war traditionell der wichtigste Hafen für den ägyptischen Seehandel mit Phönizien und Syrien gewesen.

Reiches genauso abwechseln, wie ich dies etwa für die Darstellung der Religionsgeschichte Israels gefordert habe (Albertz 1995b: 20). Ziel jeder Rekonstruktion antiker Geschichte, die mehr sein will als die Verwahrung einer Leiche im Keller, muß eine lebendige Erzählung sein, welche die Mentalitätsgeschichte voll mit in die Darstellung der sozialen und politischen Geschichte einbezieht.

Literatur und Abkürzungen

Albertz, R.

1995a   'Hat die Theologie des Alten Testaments doch noch eine Chance? Abschließende Stellungnahme in Leuven', *JBTh* 10: 177-87.

1995b   'Religionsgeschichte Israels oder Theologie des Alten Testaments! Plädoyer für eine forschungsgeschichtliche Umorientierung', *JBTh* 10: 3-24.

1996–97   *Religionsgeschichte Israels in alttestamentlicher Zeit* (2 Bde.; GAT, 8.1-2; Göttingen: Vandenhoeck & Ruprecht).

Barstad, H.M.

1996   *The Myth of the Empty Land: A Study in the History and Archaeology of Judah during the 'Exilic' Period* (Symbolae osloenses 28: Oslo: Scandinavian University Press).

Beaulieu, P.-A.

1989   *The Reign of Nabonidus: King of Babylon 556–539* (YNER, 10; New Haven: Yale University Press).

Burstein, S.M.

1978   *The Babylonaica of Berossos* (SANE, 1.5; Malibu: Undena Publisher).

Gerardi, P.

1986   'Declaring War in Mesopotamia', *AfO* 33: 30-38.

Grayson, A.K.

1975a   *Assyrian and Babylonian Chronicles* (TCS, 5; Locust Valley, NY: J.J. Augustin).

1975b   *Babylonian Historical-Literary Texts* (Toronto Semitic Texts and Studies, 3; Toronto: University of Toronto Press).

James, T.H.G.

1991   *Egypt: The Twenty-fifth and Twenty-sixth Dynasties* (CAH, 3.2; Cambridge: Cambridge University Press, 2nd edn): 677-747.

Katzenstein, H.J.

1973   *The History of Tyre: From the Beginning of the Second Millennium B.C.E. until the Fall of the Neo-Babylonian Empire in 538 B.C.E.* (Jerusalem: The Schocken Institute for Jewish Research of the Jewish Theological Seminary of America).

Langdon, S., and R. Zehnpfund

1912   *Die Neubabylonischen Königsinschriften* (Leipzig: J.C. Hinrichs).

Mayer, W.

1995   *Politik und Kriegskunst der Assyrer* (Abhandlungen zur Literatur Alt-Syriens und Mesopotamiens, 9; Münster: Ugarit Verlag).

Röllig, W.

1964   'Erwägungen zu den neuen Stelen Nabonids', *ZA* 56: 218-60.

Toorn, K. van der

1996   *Family Religion in Babylonia, Syria and Israel: Continuity and Change in the Forms of Religious Life* (Studies in the History and Culture of the Ancient Near East, 7; Leiden: E.J. Brill).

Unger, E.

1970   *Babylon: Die heilige Stadt nach der Beschreibung der Babylonier* (Berlin: W. de Gruyter, 2nd edn).

Weidner, E.F.

1939   'Jojachin, König von Juda in babylonischen Keilinschriften', in *Mélanges Syriens offerts à Monsieur René Dussaud* (Paris: Paul Geuthner): II, 923-35.

Zadok, R.

1979   *The Jews in Babylonia during the Chaldean and Achaemenian Periods According to the Babylonian Sources* (Studies in the History of the Jewish People and the Land of Israel Monograph Series, 3; Haifa: University of Haifa).

1984   'Some Jews in Babylonian Documents', *JQR* 74: 294-97.

EZRA'S RE-ENACTMENT OF THE EXILE

Bob Becking

'De enige manier om de wereld te begrijpen', zei Magnus ooit, 'is door een verhaal te vertellen. De wetenschap', zei Magnus, 'brengt alleen kennis van de werking der dingen. Verhalen brengen begrip.'

Marcel Möring[1]

Introduction[2]

Basically, a distinction should be made between two ideas: (1) the idea of history; and (2) the idea of the past. 'Past' refers to the period of time up to now. Since we experience time—or phrased in a more Kantian way, since time is the precondition for our experience—it is undeniable that there has been a past. Since time is irreversible[3] it is impossible to enter the past. This implies that any historical reconstruction is tentative and can never be tested experimentally. This fundamental observation does not imply, however, that we cannot say anything

---

1. 'The only way to understand the world', Magnus once said, 'is by telling a story. Science', Magnus said, 'only brings knowledge about how things are working. Stories supply understanding'; Marcel Möring, *In Babylon* (Amsterdam: Meulenhoff, 1997), p. 85. The 'Babylon' in this novel is an old family estate in a remote part of the country where the main character, Nathan, a fairy-tale storyteller, and Nina, his younger niece, are caught by a snowstorm. Nathan is passing the time by relating, in bits and pieces, the story of their Jewish family. Nina tries to leave the building several times, but she has to stay in Babylon until the snow has gone and/or until the story has been told.

2. Since this paper touches on a variety of topics, it is more than possible that I have overlooked important contributions on several of the issues. I do apologize for that. An informative survey of the present state of research has been given by T.C. Eskenazi, 'Current Perspectives on Ezra–Nehemiah and the Persian Period', *Currents in Research: Biblical Studies* 1 (1993), pp. 59-86.

3. See, e.g., the essays in R. Flood and M. Lockwood, *The Nature of Time* (Oxford: Basil Blackwell, 1986).

about events that have, as we assume, taken place in the past. 'History' is the reconstruction of events or strings of events that have taken place in the past. There is not just one 'history', but a whole set of competing histories. These 'histories' do not differ that much for the fact that they are based on different so-called facts. 'Histories', that is, the descriptions of a reconstruction of a part of the past, differ since they are the product of the mind of the historian. This difference can also be seen, especially, when it comes to the *Gattung*, 'a history of Israel'. Today there are a variety of concepts that differ since their authors are biased by faith, or the lack of it, or have different social or political agendas. A debate between these concepts should be based on a discussion of the relevant evidence and on the internal consistency of the various concepts. A reconstruction of the past should be evidence related and may not contain inconsistencies.[4]

In this paper I will not discuss the idea of 'Babylonian Exile' in its entirety. After a few preliminary remarks on the concept, I will confine myself to one piece of evidence: the book of Ezra. I have chosen this book for several reasons. First, I have been invited to write a commentary on Ezra and Nehemiah. As a scholar living in the neo-liberal economized world of scholarship I am forced to combine research interests. Second, it is generally held that the book of Ezra gives details on the string of events called 'exile' that does not occur elsewhere; for instance, the fact that the area surrounding Jerusalem remained populated during the period under consideration.[5] When reading the book of Ezra, I will posit the question: What kind of evidence does this text contain?

---

4. See, e.g., R.G. Collingwood, *The Idea of History: Revised Edition with Lectures 1926–1928* (Oxford: Oxford University Press, 1994); M. Stanford, *The Nature of Historical Knowledge* (Oxford: Basil Blackwell, 1987); E.A. Knauf, 'From History to Interpretation', in D.V. Edelman, *The Fabric of History: Text, Artifact and Israel's Past* (JSOTSup, 127; Sheffield: JSOT Press, 1991), pp. 26-64; H.M. Barstad, 'History and the Hebrew Bible', in Lester L. Grabbe (ed.), *Can a 'History of Israel' be Written?* (European Seminar in Historical Methodology, 1; JSOTSup, 245; Sheffield: Sheffield Academic Press, 1997), pp. 37-64.

5. See Hans M. Barstad, *The Myth of the Empty Land: A Study in the History and Archaeology of Judah during the 'Exilic' Period* (Symbolae osloenses, 28; Oslo: Scandinavian University Press, 1996), p. 44. It is rather strange to read on p. 39 of this monograph that Barstad seems to count the books of Ezra and Nehemiah as reflecting also the opposite view that 'the whole country lay desolate for seventy years'. Both statements, that on p. 39 and that on p. 44, are not argued with textual evidence!

There I will try to make some fundamental remarks concerning historiography.

The Idea of the Exile

With the idea of exile I refer to a movement in sixth-century BCE Judah. It cannot seriously be denied that in the beginning of that century inhabitants of Jerusalem and its vicinity were deported against their will to Babylonia. The Old Testament gives contradictory numbers of those deported.[6] Evidence for this deportation can be found outside the biblical discourse. A Babylonian chronicle—to be discussed below—refers to the deportation of the king of Judah. A group of cuneiform inscriptions from the sixth century BCE contains assignment lists concerning rations of food for the king [*Ia*] *'ú-kinu/Ia-ku-ú-ki-nu* = **Yahukin*,[7] his 5 sons and 13 other Judaeans.[8] These inscriptions give evidence that the king and some people from the court, at least, were deported to Babylonia. For comparable reasons it cannot seriously be denied that towards the end of the sixth century BCE persons from Babylonia started to move to an area under Persian administration called Yehud.[9] In other words, in this paper 'exile' refers to the so-called Babylonian exile. I have consciously phrased the historical framework of this exile vaguely. I have done this for at least three reasons.

6. 2 Kgs 24.14-16 mentions 18,000 deportees after the first conquest of Jerusalem. Jer. 52.28 gives the number of 3023 for this occasion; Jer. 52.29 numbers 832 deportees for the year 586 BCE, while Jer. 52.30 mentions the deportation of another 745 Judahites at an occasion not referred to elsewhere in the Old Testament. There exists, as can be imagined, an ongoing discussion among scholars with regard to these contradictory figures.

7. See R. Zadok, *The Jews of Babylonia during the Chaldean and Achaemenian Periods According to the Babylonian Sources* (Studies in the History of the Jewish People and the Land of Israel Monograph Series, 3; Haifa: University of Haifa, 1979), pp. 19-20.

8. E.F. Weidner (ed.), 'Jojachin, König von Juda in babylonischen Keilinschriften', in *Mélanges Syriens offerts à Monsieur René Dussaud* (Paris: J. Gabalda, 1939), pp. 923-35.

9. Archaeological data hint at an increase of the population in Judah/Yehud in the beginning of the 'Persian Period' by about 25 per cent; see M. Kochavi (ed.), *Judaea, Samaria and the Golan: Archaeological Survey 1967–1968* (in modern Hebrew; Jerusalem: The Survey of Israel, 1972).

(1) The year of the beginning of the Babylonian exile is unclear. Apart from the ongoing discussion on the year of Nebuchadnezzar's devastation of Jerusalem, either in 587 or 586 BCE,[10] it should be noted that the book of Kings mentions two conquests of Jerusalem followed by deportations: 2 Kgs 24.10-15 during the short reign of Jehojachin and 2 Kgs 25.1-22 in the ninth year of the reign of Zedekiah. The Babylonian Chronicles mention only one conquest. Chronicle BM 21946 Rev. 11-13 reads as follows:

> Year 7: in Kislev the king of Babylonia called out his army and marched to Hattu. He set his camp against the city of Judah and on the second of Adar he took the city and captured the king. He appointed a king of his choosing there, took heavy tribute and returned to Babylon.[11]

(2) It is also not clear when the exile ended. I will not exclude beforehand the possibility that soon after the capture of Babylon by Cyrus descendants of former Judaeans returned to their land. The Old Testament refers to an edict stemming from the first year of Cyrus in which he summoned the people to rebuild the house of YHWH in Jerusalem (2 Chron. 36.22-23; Ezra 1.1-2). A superficial reading of the book of Ezra suggests an early return from the exile. There are, however, no sources from the Persian court that independently support the

---

10. For recent treatments see A. Malamat, 'The Twilight of Judah', in J.A. Emerton (ed.), *Congress Volume, Edinburgh 1974* (VTSup, 28; Leiden: E.J. Brill, 1975), pp. 123-45; J.R. Bartlett, 'Edom and the Fall of Jerusalem, 587 B.C.', *PEQ* 114 (1982), pp. 13-24; C. Hardmeier, *Prophetie im Streit vor dem Untergang Judas: Erzählkommunikative Studien zur Entstehungssituation der Jesaja- und Jeremiaerzählungen in II Reg 18-20 und Jer 37–40* (BZAW, 187; Berlin: W. de Gruyter, 1990), pp. 247-86; G. Galil, 'The Babylonian Calendar and the Chronology of the Last Kings of Judah', *Bib* 72 (1991), pp. 367-78; O. Edwards, 'The Year of Jerusalem's Destruction', *ZAW* 104 (1992), pp. 101-106; G. Galil, *The Chronology of the Kings of Israel and Judah* (SHANE, 9; Leiden: E.J. Brill, 1996), pp. 108-26; Barstad, *The Myth of the Empty Land*, p. 13 n. 2.

11. D.J. Wiseman, *Chronicles of the Chaldaean Kings (626–556 B.C.) in the British Museum* (London: British Museum, 1956), plates v, xiv-xv, pp. 66-75; A.K. Grayson, *Assyrian and Babylonian Chronicles* (Texts from Cuneiform Sources, 5; Locust Valley, NY: J.J. Augustin, 1975), pp. 87, 99-102; for a recent translation see A.R. Millard in W.W. Hallo (ed.), *The Context of Scripture. I. Canonical Compositions from the Biblical World* (Leiden: E.J. Brill, 1997), pp. 467-68.

historical claims in the book of Ezra. The Cyrus cylinder[12] has been interpreted as showing a liberal policy of respect towards other religions. The inscription would make clear that Cyrus's policy towards the Jews was not unique but fitted the pattern of his rule.[13] Kuhrt, however, has made clear that the inscription is of a propagandistic and stereotypical nature.[14] The text reflects the world-view of the Marduk priests of the Esagila temple at Babylon. They present Cyrus as a 'good prince' replacing the 'bad prince' Nabonidus. The return of divine images and people related in Cyrus cylinder 30–34, if not mere propaganda, refers to measures taken on a rather local scale. It is divine images from cities surrounding Babylon that are brought back to the shrines from where they were exiled by Nabonidus. This passage has nothing to do with Judaeans, Jews or Jerusalem.[15] The famous Bisitun inscription of Darius[16] in its various versions relates his rebellion and rise to power but does not contain historical data on the return to Jerusalem nor the rebuilding of the temple.

12. See the most recent edition by P.-R. Berger, 'Der Kyros-Zylinder mit dem Zusatzfragment BIN II Nr. 32 und die akkadische Personennamen im Danielbuch', *ZA* 64 (1975), pp. 192-234.

13. For this point of view see, e.g., E.J. Bickermann, 'The Edict of Cyrus in Ezra 1', *JBL* 65 (1946), pp. 249-75 (Studies in Jewish and Christian History, 1; Leiden: E.J. Brill, 1976, pp. 72-108); P.R. Ackroyd, *Exile and Restoration: A Study on Hebrew Thought in the Sixth Century BC* (London: SCM Press, 1968), pp. 140-41; J.P. Weinberg, 'Demographische Notizen zur Geschichte der nachexilischen Gemeinde in Juda', *Klio* 54 (1972), pp. 45-99, quoted after the translation in J.P. Weinberg, *The Citizen–Temple Community* (JSOTSup, 151; Sheffield: JSOT Press, 1992), p. 40; T.C. Young, 'Cyrus', *ABD* 1 (1992), pp. 1231-32.

14. A. Kuhrt, 'The Cyrus Cylinder and Achaemenid Imperial Policy', *JSOT* 25 (1983), pp. 83-97.

15. Kuhrt, 'Cyrus Cylinder', pp. 87-88.

16. Aramaic version: *The Bisitun Inscription of Darius the Great Aramaic Version: Text, Translation and Commentary* (eds. J.C. Greenfield and B. Porten; Corpus inscriptionum iranicarum, I, IV; London: Lund Humphries, 1982). Babylonian version: *The Bisitun Inscription of Darius the Great Babylonian Version* (ed. E.N. von Voigtlander; Corpus inscriptionum iranicarum, I, II; London: Lund Humphries, 1978). Elamite version: F.H. Weissbach, *Die Keilinschriften der Achämeniden* (VAB, 3; Leipzig: Hinrichs, 1911). Old Persian version: *The Bisitun Inscription of Darius the Great Old Persian Text* (ed. R. Schmidt; Corpus inscriptionum iranicarum, I, I; London: Lund Humphries, 1978).

From a historical point of view, it is most probable to assume 'the return' consisted of a process of waves that lasted for more than a century.[17] Hoglund has argued rather convincingly that the various waves of return should be related to general political measures of the Persian empire: a process of ruralization in the sixth century BCE and trade oriented measures in the fifth century BCE.[18]

(3) It is unclear whether there was an ethnic continuity. Were the 'returnees' the offspring of those who once were deported? It is striking to see that the list of returners in Ezra 2[19] contains some non-Israelite names and only a few names with a Yahwistic theophoric element, which seems to indicate either a breach with pre-exilic habits or ethnic discontinuity. Particularly intriguing is the interpretation by Weinberg of this list. In his view, Neh. 7.7-69 gives the original form of the list —the purpose of which is not to describe all those returning from Mesopotamia, but should be interpreted as an indication of the collectives belonging to the 'citizen–temple community' until the years 458–457 BCE. This community consists of descendants of those returning from Mesopotamia from the edict of Cyrus onwards.[20] In another article, Weinberg investigated the question whether the members of the *bāttê ābôt*, which formed the citizen–temple community in the sixth to fourth centuries BCE, were rooted in pre-exilic milieus. He arrives at the conclusion that this question should be answered in an affirmative way for about half of the persons and groups mentioned in the lists of Ezra 2 and Nehemiah 7.[21] Since his main argument—a comparison of

17. See, e.g., Weinberg, *Citizen–Temple Community*, p. 41; Lester L. Grabbe, *Judaism from Cyrus to Hadrian* (Minneapolis: Fortress Press, 1992; London: SCM Press, 1994), pp. 126-40; P.R. Davies, *In Search of 'Ancient Israel'* (JSOTSup, 148: Sheffield, JSOT Press, 2nd edition, 1994), pp. 80-82.

18. K. Hoglund, 'The Achaemenid Context', in P.R. Davies (ed.), *Second Temple Studies. I. Persian Period* (JSOTSup, 117; Sheffield: JSOT Press, 1991), pp. 54-72; esp. pp. 57-59, 63-64.

19. I will not enter here into the question whether Neh. 7 served as a source for Ezra 2 or the other way around, or that both lists were dependent on 1 Esd. 5 or older independent material. For a discussion see H.G.M. Williamson, *Ezra, Nehemiah* (WBC, 16; Waco, TX: Word Books, 1985), pp. 28-32, 267-69.

20. Weinberg, *Citizen–Temple Community*, pp. 41-43.

21. J.P. Weinberg, 'Das *Bēit 'Ābōt* im 6.-4. Jh. v.u.Z.', *VT* 23 (1973), pp. 400-414, quoted after the translation in Weinberg, *Citizen–Temple Community*, pp. 49-61.

the personal names in the list with personal names known from else-where in the Old Testament and in epigraphic material—is only re-ferred to but not given in his paper, it would require a new investigation in order to decide whether or not Weinberg is correct. His main point, however, is that there would be a partial continuation of pre-exilic Judah.

The occurrence of Zerubbabel and Jeshua in Ezra 3.2, 8 and 5.2 might also indicate a continuity, even if of the administrative elite. Zerubbabel, for instance, is presented at Ezra 3.2 as the 'son of Sheal-tiel'. 1 Chron. 3.17 mentions Shealtiel as a son of the Judahite king Jechoniah (= Jehoiachin). The alleged continuity, however, is made problematical by the fact that the same verse, 1 Chron. 3.17, mentions Pedaiah and not Shealtiel as the father of Zerubbabel. It should be noted that the author of Ezra 3 does not stress the possible royal lineage of Zerubbabel.

(4) It is unclear what events have taken place in Judah and Jerusalem during the period under consideration. Janssen assumes the existence of a religious community during the exilic period that was responsible for the editing of the so-called Deuteronomistic history, the book of Lam-entation and a variety of prophetic passages.[22] Barstad has convinc-ingly made clear that the area was not uninhabited and that life went on as normal to some degree.[23] But it is not clear, at least to me, whether a cultural and religious continuity can be assumed.

It should be remarked that classical Hebrew has no single term for the whole process of exile and return. The nouns *go(ô)lâ* and *gālût* both refer to the exile from Israel and Judah or to the situation of the dias-pora. At no instance is the return from the diaspora also implied. The same holds for Aramaic **gālû* as attested in Daniel, Ezra and the Dead Sea Scrolls. Although the verb *šûb* is used to depict the act of return, for instance at Ezra 2.1, there is no Hebrew noun that expresses the idea of 'return'. It is impossible, from a methodological perspective, to deduce historical implications from these semantic and linguistic obser-vations. They nevertheless suggest that the idea of exile and return as a continuous process was not yet a fixed idea in pre-Hellenistic times.

---

22. E. Janssen, *Juda in der Exilszeit: Ein Beitrag zur Frage der Entstehung des Judentums* (FRLANT, 69; Göttingen: Vandenhoeck & Ruprecht, 1956).

23. Barstad, *The Myth of the Empty Land*; see also T. Willi, *Juda–Jehud–Israel: Studien zum Selbstverständnis des Judentums in persischer Zeit* (Forschungen zum Alten Testament, 12; Tübingen, J.C.B. Mohr, 1995), pp. 21-26.

The Book of Ezra

I read the book of Ezra as a composition on its own. As has been shown by Williamson there is no need to construe Ezra as part of a so-called Chronistic history writing.[24] Neither do I construe Ezra as part of a composition Ezra and Nehemiah.[25] The book of Ezra presents itself, in

24. See the arguments in S. Japhet, 'The Supposed Common Authorship of Chronicles and Ezra–Nehemiah Investigated Anew', *VT* 18 (1968), pp. 330-71; H.G.M. Williamson, *Israel in the Book of Chronicles* (Cambridge: Cambridge University Press, 1977), esp. pp. 1-70; T.C. Eskenazi, *In an Age of Prose: A Literary Approach to Ezra–Nehemiah* (SBLMS, 36; Atlanta: Scholars Press, 1988), pp. 14-36. *Pace* the classical position that can already be found in the Talmud *b. B. Bat.* 15a; but first scientifically elaborated by L. Zunz, *Die gottesdienstliche Vorträge der Juden, historisch entwickelt: Ein Beitrag zur Altertumskunde- und biblischen Kritik, zur Literatur und Religionsgeschichte* (Berlin: Louis Lamm, 1832), pp. 21-32, 303-305; and later still in an almost canonical form by M. Noth, *Überlieferungsgeschichtliche Studien: Die sammelnden und bearbeitenden Geschichtswerke im Alten Testament* (Darmstadt: Wissenschaftliche Buchgesellschaft, 3rd edition, 1967), pp. 110-216. In spite of the arguments of, e.g., Japhet and Williamson, the common authorship of Chronicles–Ezra–Nehemiah has been defended by A.H.J. Gunneweg, *Esra* (KAT; Gütersloh: Gerd Mohn, 1985), pp. 24-26; J. Blenkinsopp, *Ezra–Nehemiah* (OTL; London: SCM Press, 1988), pp. 47-54; K. Koch, 'Weltordnung und Reichsidee im alten Iran und ihre Auswirkungen auf die Provinz Jehud', in P. Frei and K. Koch, *Reichsidee und Reichsorganisation im Perserreich* (OBO, 55; Freiburg: Universitätsverlag; Göttingen: Vandenhoeck & Ruprecht, 2nd rev. edn, 1996), pp. 220-39. A. Gelston, 'The End of Chronicles', *SJOT* 10 (1996), pp. 53-60, has defended the thesis that Ezra 1–6 originally formed the end of the book of Chronicles. The material was later reused in writing the complex Ezra–Nehemiah. On Zunz, who had studied with De Wette, see H.-J. Bechtold, *Die jüdische Bibelkritik im 19. Jahrhundert* (Stuttgart: W. Kohlhammer, 1995), pp. 64-89; K. Peltonen, *History Debated: The Historical Reliability of Chronicles in Pre-Critical and Critical Research* (Publications of the Finnish Exegetical Society, 64; Helsinki: Finnish Exegetical Society; Göttingen: Vandenhoeck & Ruprecht, 1996), pp. 128-29 n. 160.

25. Against the view of a common redaction for Ezra and Nehemiah, as expressed by, for instance, Williamson, *Ezra, Nehemiah*, pp. xxxiii-xxxv; H.G.M. Williamson, *Ezra and Nehemiah* (OTG; Sheffield: JSOT Press, 1987), pp. 37-47; Eskenazi, *Age of Prose*, pp. 11-14; J.R. Shaver, 'Ezra and Nehemiah: On the Theological Significance of Making Them Contemporaries', in E. Ulrich, J.W. Wright, R.P. Carroll and P.R. Davies (eds.), *Priests, Prophets and Scribes: Essays on the Formation of Second Temple Judaism in Honour of Joseph Blenkinsopp* (JSOTSup, 149; Sheffield: JSOT Press, 1992), pp. 76-86, esp. p. 85; see the

its present form, as a composition on its own that should be read as a composition on its own.

In my view the book consists of three narratives:[26] (1) Ezra 1–2 relates the movement of a group of people from 'being in Babylonia' to 'living in Jerusalem and vicinity'. (2) Ezra 3–6 is to be seen as a coherent narrative—the main narrative programme of which can be labelled as the abolition of the non-celebration of the Passover. The (re)building of the temple, the change from 'altar' to 'temple' is an embedded narrative programme, apparently necessarily for the celebration of the Passover. (3) The story of Ezra's coming to Jerusalem and the measures taken by him (Ezra 7–10). In the present form of the book of Ezra these three narratives are related in a consecutive order suggesting that the 'events' narrated took place in the narrated order: return in the time of Cyrus; rebuilding of the temple under Darius; and reorganization of the community under Artaxerxes. Read in a naive way, and coordinated with the dates of the relevant Persian emperors, this sequence would supply a clear and simple picture of things that have happened. There are, however, some complicating facts. Some have to do with anomalies in the chronology internal to the text; some have to do with the problematic identification of the Persian kings referred to; and, more theoretically, some have to do with the question about the status of the data in the book of Ezra.

An anomaly in the internal chronology is related to Jeshua and Zerubbabel. They are mentioned in 3.2 as officers building the altar for the God of Israel. According to the internal chronology of Ezra this event took place in the reign of Cyrus. According to the same internal chronology Jeshua and Zerubbabel are still in charge in Ezra 5.2 where they are initiating the rebuilding of the temple of Jerusalem. This initiative took place during the reign of a Persian king named Darius who governed after Cyrus, Ahasuerus and Artaxerxes. Moreover, it took place after the exchange of letters mentioned in Ezra 4 during the reign of Ahasuerus and Artaxerxes. Within the internal chronology there is no problem with these textual features except the fact that they suppose

---

arguments in J.C. VanderKam, 'Ezra-Nehemiah or Ezra and Nehemiah?', in Ulrich *et al.* (eds.), *Priests, Prophets and Scribes,* pp. 55-75; D. Kraemer, 'On the Relationship of the Books of Ezra and Nehemiah', *JSOT* 59 (1993), pp. 73-92.

26. Applying a different theory of literature, Eskenazi, *Age of Prose,* arrives at a different view on the composition and coherence of the narratives in the book of Ezra.

either a quick change in rulership at the Persian court or a long life for
the two officials mentioned. Problems arise when this internal chronology is related to external chronology. So either Darius mentioned in
Ezra 5 is identical with Darius I Hystaspes (522–486 BCE), or he is
identical with Darius II Ochus (424–405 BCE). Both possibilities provoke problems. The historical reconstruction yielded by the first
identification problematizes the chronological order of the letters, since
in this reconstruction the correspondence in Ezra 5 took place earlier
than the exchange of letters referred to in Ezra 4. This is rather meaningless in view of the contents of the letters. Ezra 4 stops the building
of the temple while Ezra 5 gives permission to complete the building
activities. I do not see the point in a reversed historical order.[27] The
second identification mentioned supposes that Jeshua and Zerubbabel
had lived a superhumanly long time. Cyrus died in 530 BCE and Darius
II Ochus captured the Persian throne in 424 BCE. These observations
provoke the idea that the book of Ezra, or at least the narrative in Ezra
3–6, is a composite text, certainly not an eyewitness report and probably confused various events that had taken place in the past.[28]

How should one assess the data in the book of Ezra from a historiographic point of view? That is, how should the narratives in Ezra
be classified? After a first phase of critical scholarship in which the
character of Ezra was considered to be pure fiction,[29] mainstream Old
Testament scholarship—pursuing consciously or unconsciously a nineteenth-century positivistic agenda—has been looking for authentic
sources that can help to reconstruct what really happened. It was

---

27. *Pace* B. Halpern, 'A Historiographic Commentary on Ezra 1–6:
Achronological Narrative and Dual Chronology in Israelite Historiography', in
W.H. Propp, B. Halpern and D.N. Freedman (eds.), *The Hebrew Bible and its
Interpreters* (Biblical and Judaic Studies, 1; Winona Lake, IN: Eisenbrauns, 1990),
pp. 81-142; esp. pp. 103-29.

28. See also G. Garbini, *History and Ideology in Ancient Israel* (trans. John
Bowden; London: SCM Press, 1988), pp. 153-54.

29. This position is generally related to C.C. Torrey, *The Composition and
Historical Value of Ezra–Nehemiah* (BZAW, 2; Giessen: Richter Verlag, 1896);
C.C. Torrey, *Ezra Studies* (Chicago: University of Chicago Press, 1910). Torrey,
however, had predecessors in the French writers M. Vernes and E. Renan (See
Garbini, *History and Ideology*, p. 154). After the rise of the Albright school this
position has been abandoned with the exception of Garbini, *History and Ideology*,
p. 155; Davies, *In Search of 'Ancient Israel'*, p. 83; see below R.P. Carroll, pp. 73-
77.

thought that, somehow, the book of Ezra in its present composite form, is to be seen as a compilation of a variety of sources. A range of propositions have been made.[30] Williamson, for instance, accepts that Ezra 7–10 is a reworking of an older narrative that might go back to a Jerusalem copy of Ezra's report for the Persian king; furthermore, he assumes that the Aramaic letters in Ezra 4–6 are authentic and that the decree of Cyrus (1.2-4) and the inventory of temple vessels (1.9-11) reflect authentic sources.[31] Halpern[32] in a very learned article considers Ezra 1.1–4.3 as containing authentic material from the reign of Cyrus. In his conception, Ezra 4.4–6.22 is written in a form comparable to the so-called summary-inscriptions of the Mesopotamian kings.[33] This would imply that the material in the textual unit under consideration is not ordered chronologically but geographically, thus distorting the narrative order. Halpern claims that we have authentic material from different periods and concludes with the following historical reconstruction: The return from exile, ordered by Cyrus in 538 BCE, eventually took place in 521 BCE. The rebuilding of the temple started in the reign of Darius (I) in 520 BCE and was completed in 515 BCE. The obstruction of 'the neighbours' (Ezra 4.4-5) would refer to hostilities between 538 and 520 BCE. The obstructions mentioned in Ezra 4.6-23 would refer to events in the reigns of Xerxes and Artaxerxes.

This line of thought is, apparently, based on the idea that it is the task of the historian to look for original sources and eyewitness reports and,

30. For a survey see Williamson, *Ezra and Nehemiah*, pp. 14-36; to which should be added G.W. Ahlström, *The History of Ancient Palestine from the Palaeolithic Period to Alexander's Conquest* (JSOTSup, 146; Sheffield: JSOT Press, 1993), pp. 812-88; Koch, 'Weltordnung und Reichsidee', pp. 206-94.

31. Williamson, *Ezra, Nehemiah*, see at the various passages; Williamson, *Ezra and Nehemiah*, pp. 20-26, 29-34.

32. Halpern, 'Historiographic Commentary'.

33. Halpern, 'Historiographic Commentary', pp. 111-12; note that Halpern is not giving a comprehensive description of this *Gattung* that differs from the Royal Annals; for a form-critical description of the 'summary-inscription' see, e.g., H. Tadmor, 'The Historical Inscriptions of Adad-Nirari III', *Iraq* 35 (1973), pp. 141-50 (141); N. Na'aman, 'The Brook of Egypt and Assyrian Policy on the Border of Egypt', *Tel Aviv* 6 (1979), pp. 68-90 (68 n. 2); K.L. Younger, *Ancient Conquest Accounts: A Study in Ancient Near Eastern and Biblical History Writing* (JSOTSup, 98; Sheffield: JSOT Press, 1990), p. 290 n. 99; S.A. Irvine, *Isaiah, Ahaz, and the Syro-Ephraimitic Crisis* (SBLDS, 123; Atlanta: Scholars Press, 1990), p. 26.

in case these are not available, to reconstruct them from the existing texts and data. These sources can help to reconstruct 'what really happened'. It should be noted that this is an obsolete way of doing history, for three reasons. (1) In order to 'save' the historicity of (parts of) the biblical tradition, it leads to historical anomalies. For instance, in the reconstruction of Halpern two anomalies are observable. He accepts that the rebuilding of the temple was already finished by the time that opposition to the building arose. I do not see the historical point of mentioning obstructions to the building of a sanctuary that is already completed. In his outline of the events behind the text, he proposes that the following two events took place in the reign of Cyrus: (a) 'gathering of rebuilding materials' (Ezra 3.7); (b) 'rebuff of neighbours' (Ezra 4.1-3). He dates these events in the years 521 and 520 BCE.[34] By that time Cyrus has been dead for almost a decade. His son Cambyses was also dead, and Darius was reigning over the empire. Thus, in order to 'save' the historicity of an early return from exile and a quick rebuilding of the temple, Halpern has to accept these historical anomalies. (2) It does not account for the fact that the literary-critical operations as implied in this approach are tentative and hypothetical. (3) It is based on the somewhat naive view that 'text' minus 'ideology' equals 'history'. Williamson, and others, seems to believe that when we subtract the religious view from the book of Ezra, we have objective knowledge about the past at our disposal.

Recently a new approach has emerged. Provoked by the ideas in the commentary of Gunneweg,[35] Grabbe has problematized the authenticity of the sources underlying the book of Ezra.[36] Grabbe questions the authenticity of the Aramaic documents, the letters in Ezra 5–6, and the Ezra Memoir (Ezra 7–10). His main argument runs, as far as I can see, as follows. First, the comparative material by which to judge the authenticity of the 'archive material' is too small in number and of uncertain authenticity. We simply have too few contemporary letters and archival notes to conclude whether or not the 'Edict of Cyrus' and the Aramaic letters in the book of Ezra are genuine or not. Second, he argues that in case it can be proven that the material in Ezra goes back

---

34. Halpern, 'Historiographic Commentary', p. 125.

35. Gunneweg, *Esra*.

36. L.L. Grabbe. 'Reconstructing History from the Book of Ezra', in Davies (ed.), *Second Temple Studies. I. Persian Period*, pp. 98-107; see also Grabbe, *Judaism from Cyrus to Hadrian*, pp. 30-41.

to genuine documents, we do not possess these documents. He quite correctly remarks that we have the material embedded in the narratives and thus in a reworked form. He even gives a few examples from Josephus for his thesis that 'doctoring of documents to make them more pro-Jewish seems to have been a minor cottage industry', by which is meant that editorial intervention and embedding in a narrative can change the scope and the ideology of a document to such a degree that it is impossible to reconstruct the original text.[37] If one prefers to do so, Grabbe's position can be labelled as 'sceptical' or 'minimalistic'.[38] My criticism of his position, however, has nothing to do with this kind of classification. My problem is that he still accepts the book of Ezra as a source and that he seems to opt for the possibility of an objective reconstruction of events that have taken place in the past.[39] To tackle the issue at stake a more methodical approach is needed.

The methodical mistake made by source-oriented historians, regardless of their being minimalists or maximalists, is that they identify the source under consideration with 'what really happened'. Therefore, I would again like to stress that 'a text' is not 'the event'. A text is a description of reality and does not equal reality except from the fact that a text is a reality on its own, but that is a different point. An example from daily life might illuminate this: A newspaper report on the *Tour de France* is not identical with the heroic cycling tour. The newspaper gives the reporter's view of the event. He[40] is making a biased selection from a large number of smaller and more important events and presents that selection in a narrative form. The same holds for the book of Ezra. The text in its present form is not the past and is not identical with an event or a string of events that might have taken place in the past. The text is a relic of the past and as such it is a piece of evidence.[41] The question, however, is the status of the evidence. Two remarks, I think, must be made. (1) A text is a piece of evidence about its author, his or her views and the period in which the text was written.

---

37. Grabbe, 'Reconstructing History', pp. 101-102.

38. Grabbe seems to expect this kind of classification; cf. 'Reconstructing History', pp. 105-106.

39. I infer this from the historiographically optimistic tone in a section in his paper headed 'Where do we go from here?'; Grabbe, 'Reconstructing History', pp. 103-104.

40. Only sometimes 'she'.

41. Collingwood, *Idea of History*.

(2) A narrative text is not mere evidence about the 'events' narrated—its story is a history on its own. Both remarks will now be elaborated.

(1) The book of Ezra is not only a book *on* 'history', but also a book *in* history. The author is narrating the past, most probably arranging and rearranging 'facts' and events, most probably rewriting and restyling documents (if not inventing!), but not for the sake of the past as such. His aim is apparently not to supply the reader something as verifiable knowledge of the past, although he presents the events as real events. The main thing is that he is narrating the past in view of his present situation. Thus, the question arises: Do we know anything about the 'present situation' of the author of the book of Ezra? Unfortunately, not very much. Two things, however, are clear. (1) Since Darius (II Ochus) is the last Persian king referred to in Ezra 3–6, I would suggest that Ezra's mission (Ezra 7–10) should be related to the reign of Artaxerxes II Memnon (404–359 BCE).[42] This would imply that the narratives cannot be earlier than the fourth century BCE. (2) The Persian period is characterized by a multitude of Judaisms. Various forms of this religion are competing. In my view the book of Ezra, or at least Ezra 3–6, has been written as a legitimation of one form of Judaism. Other forms of Judaism or maybe Proto-Samaritanism are depicted as adversaries. The narratives claim that this form of Judaism, which focused on the celebration of the Passover in the Jerusalemite temple, is the only form with both divine and imperial support. Thus, the narratives in Ezra function as a self-definition of one stream of Judaism in the final decades of the Persian period.[43]

(2) Collingwood has developed a hermeneutic of history in which the idea of re-enactment plays an important role.[44] This has to do with the inaccessibility of the past. To overcome this problem the historian has to re-enact the past in his or her mind. Within the limits of the human mind a part of the past is re-enacted—turned into a play, so to say. Imagination plays, by implication, an important role, but it is not mere fantasy that yields the act. First, any re-enactment is steered by the available evidence. Second, re-enactment is a way for the historian to experience the past, but it is never identical with the past.

42. See thus Ahlström, *History of Ancient Palestine*, p. 880.

43. See also P.R. Davies, 'Scenes from the Early History of Judaism', in D.V. Edelman (ed.), *The Triumph of Elohim: From Yahwisms to Judaisms* (CBET, 13; Kampen: Kok, 1995), pp. 145-82.

44. Collingwood, *Idea of History*, esp. pp. 282-302.

This re-enactment generally takes the form of a narrative. Most histories are written in the narrative form. This holds both for boring textbooks used in secondary education and for the well-informed books by Le Roy Ladurie.[45] The idea of 'narrative' is not totally identical with the idea of 'fiction'. The identification, often made in biblical scholarship, creates a pitfall as well as a dead-end street. They are different categories. 'Narrative' is a meta-syntactical idea by which texts can be classified. It hints at the form, *Gattung*, of the text and the tenses used in it. 'Fiction' has to do with the question about how far away from reality a text stands. For example, a restaurant bill prepared by a drunken waiter and containing various miscalculations does not have a narrative form but can still be classified as fiction. With regard to stories in the Hebrew Bible, the fact that many, if not all, of them are related using the narrative chain does not imply that they are narrating fiction. External evidence must be decisive on this point.[46]

To bring this point to a more fundamental discussion, I will refer to the narrativism of Danto and Ankersmit.[47] For them the *narratio* is a form of history-writing (or re-enactment) that consciously selects and connects 'events' from the past into a narrative. The historian, by profession, is responsible for the selection of the material and the connection of data. When history-writing takes the form of a narrative, it is an organization of the past and not a mere description of it. A distinction should be made between the narrative as a whole and its elements. This distinction has to do with epistemology. The narrative as such cannot be verified, since it is the product of the mind of the historian. All that can be asked is internal consistency and evidence relatedness. A narrative relating history should not be self-contradictory. The reader should be given an insight into how the elements of the narrative are related to

---

45. See esp. E. Le Roy Ladurie, *Montaillou: Village occitan de 1294 à 1324* (Paris: Editions Gallimard, 1975); *Le siècle des Platter 1499–1628*. I. *Le mendiant et le professeur* (Paris: Librairie Arthème Fayard, 1996).

46. See also the fundamental remarks by Knauf, 'From History to Interpretation', pp. 47-50, on this subject.

47. A.C. Danto, *Analytical Philosophy of History* (Cambridge: Cambridge University Press, 1968); F.R. Ankersmit, *Narrative Logic: A Semantical Analysis of the Historian's Language* (Den Haag: Mouton, 1983); see also the remarks by Barstad, 'History and the Hebrew Bible', esp. pp. 54-60.

archival data and comparable evidence.[48] The narrative, however, contains sentences or groups of sentences that are evidence related. They can be verified over and against the evidence available.[49]

All these remarks lead me to the supposition that the book of Ezra is not to be seen as a primary source or as a piece of evidence as such, but as a *narration*. The author of this book, or the group of persons responsible for it, is presenting its organization. The book of Ezra is a history competing with other histories about the same period (e.g. 1 Esdras; *Damascus Document*; Josephus; Herodotus[50]). The book of Ezra presents a biased image on the exile and its aftermath by which later fourth- or third-century BCE, cultic and political positions are defended, namely, a form of Judaism in which the festival of Passover in the temple of Jerusalem and a rather strict interpretation of the Torah play an important role. What are the elements of this image of the exile?

Ezra's Re-enactment of the Exile

As has been indicated above, the book of Ezra consists of three narratives. The 'idea of the exile' in these three narratives will now be discussed.

(1) In the first narrative, Ezra 1–2, some elements are related and some claims are made. It is related that Cyrus, king of Persia, ordered the return of exiled Judaeans. The aim of this return is the building of a temple for YHWH. Furthermore, it is narrated that non-Israelites living in Mesopotamia supported their returning neighbours with precious metals and cattle. The aim of these gifts is the forthcoming cult in the temple for YHWH. The next element is the giving back of the temple vessels previously deported from Jerusalem by Nebuchadnezzar II. These vessels are given back in order that they will serve again in the cult of the temple of YHWH. After a list of names, it is narrated that this group returned to Jerusalem and its vicinity and that offerings were made for the temple of YHWH. From the organization of the material,

---

48. See, e.g., Ankersmit, *Narrative Logic*, pp. 75-76. Here too, Le Roy Ladurie's books form a good example, since he gives the reader the possibility to control the elements of his historical stories against the evidence on which they are constructed.

49. See Ankersmit, *Narrative Logic*, pp. 29, 75, 104.

50. See on these the informative article by M.A. Knibb, 'The Exile in the Literature of the Intertestamental Period', *Heythrop Journal* 17 (1976), pp. 253-72.

two claims representing the view of the narrator are clear. First, the whole of the process of return took place on divine initiative and imperial guidance. Second, a continuity with pre-exilic features is made. This becomes clear at two instances in the narrative. Of the vessels, retrieved by the Persian king, it is explicitly said that they are identical with the vessels taken from Jerusalem by Nebuchadnezzar II (Ezra 1.7).[51] Finally, it should be noted—as Thomas Willi has observed—that the 'exile' is not presented here as a historical feature standing on its own, but as the prologemenon to a new period.[52]

(2) Ezra 3–6 is to be seen as a coherent narrative, the main narrative programme of which can be labelled as the abolition of the non-celebration of the Passover. The (re)building of the temple, the change from 'altar' to 'temple', is an embedded narrative programme, apparently necessarily for the celebration of the Passover. Within this framework it is related that several groups were opposing the rebuilding of the temple under the leadership of Zerubbabel and Jeshua. There is, however, one group of people that wants to help the returners in building a temple in Jerusalem (Ezra 4.1-3). They present themselves as descendants of deportees brought to the area in the time of Esarhaddon, king of Assyria, and they consider themselves as worshipping the same deity as the returnees. Their help, however, is not accepted. In Ezra 4.10 another group of persons presenting themselves as descendants of exiles is mentioned. Here, a group of people brought to the Samarian area from Erech, Babylon, Susa, Elam and elsewhere by 'the great and esteemed Osnappar'[53] are among those who stand in opposition to the rebuilding activities of the Jews. The opposing groups are presented rather vaguely. The greatest opposition against the enterprise seems to come from persons involved in the Persian

51. See, e.g., P.R. Ackroyd, 'The Temple Vessels—A Continuity Theme', in J.A. Emerton (ed.), *Studies in the Religion of Ancient Israel* (VTSup, 23; Leiden: E.J. Brill, 1972), pp. 166-81.

52. Willi, *Juda–Jehud–Israel*, pp. 53-57.

53. The identity of Osnappar is not clear. Often, the name is seen as a confusion of Ashurbanipal; see Blenkinsopp, *Ezra–Nehemiah*, p. 113; A.K. Grayson, 'Osnappar', *ABD* 5 (1992), p. 50. This identification, however, is not without problems, both philological and historical: see A.R. Millard, 'Assyrian Royal Names in Biblical Hebrew', *JSS* 21 (1976), pp. 11-12; Williamson, *Ezra, Nehemiah*, p. 55. Note that Osnappar is *not* presented as a king in Ezra 4.10. He might as well have been an Assyrian, Babylonian or Persian high officer responsible for deportations.

administration, such as Bishlam, Mithredath and Tabeel (4.7); Rehum and Shimshai (4.8-23); Tattenai and Shethar-Bozenai (5.3–6.15). In Ezra 3.3 and 4.4-5 hostility between returners and 'the people of the land' is related. Within the narrative the identity of this group is not clarified. Nevertheless, it seems as if descendants of Judahites who were not exiled are being referred to. In Ezra 3.12 an interesting detail is narrated. It is claimed that some priests and Levites who had seen the pre-exilic temple were present at the ceremony after the laying of the foundation of the new temple. This is a claim of continuity. It is, however, not clear what exactly is narrated. Did the priests and Levites mentioned here belong to the group of returnees that long ago had seen the devastation of the first temple by the Babylonian forces? Or did they belong to the group that had stayed in the land? In both cases, a relation with external chronology raises the problem that these priests and Levites must have lived an extremely long time.

(3) In the third narrative Ezra, finally, appears. The story of his coming to Jerusalem and the measures taken by him is related in Ezra 7–10. These measures mainly concern the problem of the so-called mixed marriages. With regard to exile and return some interesting elements are narrated. During the reign of the Persian king Artaxerxes, a new group of Israelites is allowed to go to Jerusalem. It is interesting to note that this movement is not phrased with verbs from the semantic field 'to return', but from the field 'to come; to come up':

Ezra 7.6	Ezra came up (*'ālā*) from Babel
Ezra 7.7	Some of the Israelites and some of the priests, the Levites, the singers…came up (*wayya'ªlû*) to Jerusalem
Ezra 7.8	And he (Ezra) came (*wayyābo'*) to Jerusalem in the fifth month
Ezra 7.13	Any one of the people of Israel…who volunteers to go (*limhāk*) to Jerusalem with you may go (*yᵉhāk*) [Letter of Artaxerxes]
Ezra 7.14	You are sent by the king (*šᵉlîuhtā*)[54] …to conduct an inquiry [Letter of Artaxerxes]
Ezra 8.1	These are the heads of the families, together with their genealogy, who went up (*hāl'olîm*) with me from Babylon

---

54. MT reads *šᵉlîah*; read with the majority of the commentaries: *šᵉlîhtā*.

Ezra 8.30	Thus the priests and the Levites too responsibility for the consignment of silver and gold and vessels, to bring (*l'ḥābî'*) them to Jerusalem, to the house of our God
Ezra 8.31	We departed (*wannis'ā*) from the river Ahava
Ezra 8.32	We came to (*wannābô'*) Jerusalem

There seems to be only one exception:

| Ezra 8.35 | Those who had come (*habbā'îm*) from the captivity, the sons of the exile (*b'nê-haggôlā*), offered as burnt-offerings to the God of Israel |

It might, however, be considered that the 'sons of the exile' could be a different group from the 'Ezra-group'—an interpretation that seems to be affirmed by Ezra 10.7, where the 'sons of the exile' are presented as yet another group. For the time being I take the expression to refer to a group that came from Mesopotamia at an earlier date. Therefore, it seems appropriate to suggest that the narrator in Ezra 7–10 is not claiming continuity between pre-exilic Judaeans and members of this 'Ezra-group'.

It is interesting to note that in the list of members of the 'Ezra-group' (Ezra 8.1-14), more names with a Yahwistic theophoric element are present than in the list in Ezra 2. The narrative mentions a specific area of departure: the river (or canal) Ahava. Furthermore, the bringing of vessels to Jerusalem in order that they will serve in the temple is narrated. Contrary to the first narrative in the book of Ezra there is no claim here that these vessels were identical with the vessels carried away from Jerusalem by Nebuchadnezzar II. They are presented as newly made and part of Artaxerxes's grant to Ezra.[55] With regard to this element, too, there is no continuity.

There is no unambiguous reference to a group that had stayed in Judah and Jerusalem during the exilic period. In Ezra 9.1-2 the reader receives the impression that 'people of Israel' that have lived in an unfaithful way by mingling with several surrounding people might be the group that stayed in the land. The remark in Ezra 9.4 on the 'unfaithfulness of the exiles' shows that a group of returnees is meant. On the level of narrative organization of the past, it should be remarked that this third narrative too claims divine initiative and imperial guidance. There are no clear claims concerning continuity with pre-exilic

55. Thus Williamson, *Ezra and Nehemiah*, p. 83.

Israelites or Judaeans. Only in the genealogy of Ezra, 7.1-5, is a link with pre-exilic persons narrated.

In the present form of the book of Ezra these three narratives are related in a consecutive order suggesting that the elements narrated took place in the narrated order: return in the time of Cyrus; rebuilding of the temple under Darius; reorganization of the community under Artaxerxes. Here, the hand of the narrator organizing and coordinating elements from the past is most clearly visible. At the same time the narrator's ideology becomes clear. The reader is supposed to believe that the belief-system of the Ezra-group, in which the celebration of Passover in the temple and a faithful stand towards the Torah of YHWH play an important role, is the only acceptable, divinely willed continuation of pre-exilic Yahwism.[56] To convince the reader a selection of events from the past is narrated.

Historical Trustworthiness?

It might seem strange that I keep asking questions about the historical reliability of the elements in the Ezra narratives, but it is not. It is a part of the narrativistic approach of history writing, as elaborated by Danto and Ankersmit, that the reliability of the elements of the narrative can be explored. There is, however, one rather important problem. A modern historian, when giving his or her re-enactment of the past or relating her or his *narratio,* has to relate to the evidence. The books of Le Roy Ladurie form a good and successful example of this way of writing history. This also implies that the reader not only can enjoy the novellistic style of presentation but is also able to check the various elements of the *narratio.* When it comes to the appreciation of Ezra's re-enactment of the exile this last enterprise is very problematic, since we no longer know on which pieces of evidence the author of the book of Ezra has built his *narratio.* A literary-critical or redaction-historical approach in which earlier layers or original sources are detected is not a way out of this problem, since it will only lead to circular reasoning. Even if it were possible to reconstruct the Aramaic or Persian documents—a possibility that is debated among scholars[57]—that would

56. See also Davies, 'Scenes from the Early History of Judaism', *passim.*

57. It would be interesting to describe this discussion and to assess the arguments from both sides. See on the discussion Williamson, *Ezra and Nehemiah,* pp. 20-26, 29-36; Halpern, 'Historiographic Commentary', *passim*; Grabbe,

have served the author(s) of the book of Ezra when organizing the narratives discussed, this still does not supply us with independent external evidence. Documents reconstructed in this way are not equal to archival data.

Before making some remarks on the external evidence, it should be noted that the internal evidence in the book of Ezra is not without problems in view of a historical reconstruction. (1) As noted above, the relation between the internal and the external chronology, especially of the second narrative, is not without problems. (2) The first two narratives stress the theme of continuity between pre-exilic and postexilic features. This element is absent in the third narrative. (3) The first two narratives depict the movement from Babylon as a return from exile. This depiction is absent in the third narrative. (4) There seem to be no clear hints in the narratives on the continuous habitation of Judah in the 'exilic' period. (5) In the first two narratives the persons coming from Babylon are presented as 'Jews'. In the third narrative they are named 'Israelites'. In the lists of names of both groups a differentiation is observable with regard to the theophoric elements in the personal names. It is not clear, at least not to me, what to make of this observation on the level of history writing. It seems to open the possibility that the different waves coming from Mesopotamia had different ethnic or religious roots, some in pre-exilic Judah and some, perhaps, even in pre-exilic Samaria.

The book of Ezra is not written with footnotes. This implies that the modern reader is not certain whether the evidence with which the elements in the narratives are compared were known as such to Ezra's author. Therefore, I would classify the evidence to be discussed as circumstantial evidence. There is, unfortunately, not much circumstantial evidence. From the point of view of the Persian administration, Jerusalem and vicinity was but a remote and unimportant part of the empire.

'Reconstructing History', pp. 98-106; Grabbe, *Judaism from Cyrus to Hadrian*, pp. 30-41. See beside the commentaries on Ezra: Bickermann, 'Edict of Cyrus in Ezra 1', *passim*; G. Widengren, 'The Persian Period', in J. Hayes and J.M. Miller (eds.), *Israelite and Judaean History* (London: SCM Press, 1977), pp. 489-538; J.C.H. Lebram, 'Die Traditionsgeschichte der Ezragestalt und die Frage nach dem historischen Esra', in H. Sancisi-Weerdenburg (ed.), *Achaemenid History*. I. *Sources, Structures and Synthesis* (Proceedings of the Groningen 1983 Achaemenid History Workshop; Leiden: Nederlands Instituut voor het Nabije Oosten, 1987), pp. 103-38; Koch, 'Weltordnung und Reichsidee', pp. 210-20, 284-94.

From the time of Darius I, the satrapy 'Beyond the River' is mentioned in lists of provinces.[58] This is, however, the only—but not very informative—written evidence to be related to the book of Ezra. No copies of the letters and official documents presented in the three narratives have been unearthed. There are no inscriptions mentioning a return of a group or groups of Israelites or Judaeans to Jerusalem. Archaeological evidence, as far as I can see, hints at a cultural continuation from the Neo-Babylonian to the Persian period.[59]

In sum, although I am convinced that processes like 'exile' and 'return' have taken place, be it on a relatively small scale, the re-enactment of this part of the past in the book of Ezra has not given details that can either be classified as historically trustworthy or as untrustworthy. In fact, we know too little.

One final question: Can the book of Ezra be used for the reconstruction of a history of the so-called exilic period? My answer would be that the book of Ezra can be used for *a* reconstruction, or for *several* reconstructions of that period. If I were to write such a history, I would do it in a narrative form indicating to the reader that my story is tentative and often hypothetical and that many gaps are filled by imagination. The book of Ezra, that is, some elements from its narratives, however, would play a role in my re-enactment of the exile.

---

58. See O. Leuze, *Die Satrapieneinteilung in Syrien und im Zweistromlande von 520–320* (Halle: Max Niemeyer, 1935); A.F. Rainey, 'The Satrapy "Beyond the River"', *AJBA* 1 (1969), pp. 51-78; W.J. Vogelsang, *The Rise and Organisation of the Achaemenid Empire: The Eastern Iranian Evidence* (SHANE, 3; Leiden: E.J. Brill, 1992), pp. 96-119.

59. See E. Stern, *Material Culure of the Land of the Bible in the Persian Period 538–332 B.C.* (Warminster: Aris and Philips, 1982); H. Weippert, *Palästina in vorhellenistischer Zeit* (Handbuch der Archäologie, 2.1; Munich: C.H. Becksche Verlagsbuchhandlung, 1988), pp. 682-728; Barstad, *The Myth of the Empty Land.*

EXILE! WHAT EXILE?
DEPORTATION AND THE DISCOURSES OF DIASPORA

Robert P. Carroll

In Memoriam Ferdinand Deist[1]

What can the Flat [Earth] Error teach us about human knowledge and our own worldview? First, historians, scientists, scholars and other writers often wittingly or unwittingly repeat and propagate errors of fact or interpretation. No one can be automatically believed or trusted without checking methodology and sources. Second, scholars and scientists often are led by their biases more than by the evidence. Third, *historians, who could be expected by the nature of their trade to understand that every worldview is a human construct and that paradigms of knowledge are precarious and inevitably change, including the religious, scientific realist, and positivist worldviews, sometimes forget that there are and can be no privileged systems by which to judge the truth of other systems.* Scepticism can be applied not only to reputed facts but also to accepted theories, models, intellectual fads, views of the world. Whether God creates meaning, the cosmos creates meaning, or humanity creates meaning, meaning is both arbitrary and absolute. There is no higher meaning by which meaning can be judged.

Jeffrey Burton Russell[2]

1.   While writing this paper I learned to my horror that Ferdinand Deist had died in Heidelberg of a massive heart attack on 12 July 1997. South African biblical scholarship has lost one of its intellectual giants and, in my opinion, its finest Hebrew Bible scholar. I mourn with all his friends the loss to the new South Africa of his fine voice, sharp intelligence and radical critique of all political chicanery. As a tribute to him I dedicate this paper to his memory. On my part I shall miss greatly his genuine intellectual energy, stimulating companionship and, especially, his provocative critiques of my own work.

2.   Jeffrey Burton Russell, *Inventing the Flat Earth: Columbus and Modern Historians* (New York: Praeger, 1991), p. 75. Russell's discussion of modern beliefs about an imagined mediaeval belief in a Flat Earth provides some salutary lessons for modern historians working on beliefs about and in the past. I have

For the other truth of the matter is that exile is a metaphysical condition.
                                                    Joseph Brodsky[3]

Exile and exodus: those are the two sides or faces of the myth that shapes the subtext of the narratives and rhetoric of the Hebrew Bible. Between these twin topoi (and their mediating notion of the empty land) is framed, constructed and constituted the essential story of the Hebrew Bible. They reflect a deep narratological structure and constant concern with journeys into or out of territories. Of course, any journey out of the land or out of a country is equally a journey into a different land or country (it is a zero sum game). So *exodus equals exile or deportation* and vice versa. Adam and Eve are driven out of Eden, Cain wanders through the land of Nod, and Avram and his family leave Babylonia to go to the land of Canaan in an exodus that presages the much larger exodus from Egypt under Moses. Avram and his immediate family wander in and out of Egypt, parodying the exodus myth.[4] Jacob flees his homeland, returns to it and finally retreats to exile in Egypt to live out his life there—but is buried in the family tomb in Canaan (Genesis 49–50). Thus in his life Jacob replicates much of the history of Israel by anticipation and Genesis functions as a preface to the biblical story of Israel wherein the story is re-enacted in the life of the individual patriarch. Read Genesis in order to save yourself reading the rest of the Hebrew Bible. Joseph is taken down to Egypt, but never leaves it except in a coffin. Moses reverses Joseph's journey and life's work by taking the clans out of Egypt into the wilderness and Joshua completes what neither Joseph nor Moses could achieve by taking the clans into Canaan. Within the story of the kingdoms (Kings) there is a

added emphases to part of this citation from his stimulating little book in order to engage the attention of the participants in this historiography seminar.

3.   'The Condition We Call Exile', in Joseph Brodsky, *On Grief and Reason: Essays* (Harmondsworth: Penguin Books, 1997), p. 25.

4.   Avram's exodus in the book of Genesis may be said to presage or parody Moses' exodus in the book of Exodus or Moses' exodus could be said to complete, make symmetrical, or bring to closure Avram's pilgrimage. Of course, Avram's pilgrimage from Babylonia provides an inclusio and framing for the biblical grand narrative which now begins with an exodus *from* Babylon and ends with the deportation of the people *to* Babylon. On the notion of the exodus as pilgrimage see Mark S. Smith (with contributions by Elizabeth M. Bloch-Smith), *The Pilgrimage Pattern in Exodus* (JSOTSup, 239; Sheffield: Sheffield Academic Press, 1997).

fairly constant representation of people (groups and individuals) prac-
tising exodus or exile according to the political fortunes prevailing in
their time. The story of the kingdoms ends with the razing of the
temple, the city's sacking and the deportation of the senior citizens to
Babylon. Other groups flee to Egypt, thereby reversing the exodus. The
Chronicler adds the final touch to this narratological obsession by turning the Babylonian deportation into a fixed-term exile. *In my opinion*
exile is a biblical trope and, whether it may be treated as an event in the
real socio-economic historical world outside the text or not, it should be
treated as a fundamental element in the cultural poetics of biblical discourses. It may have historical referents, but it is as a root metaphor
that it contributes most to the biblical narrative.[5]

I would also want to add a further point: history notwithstanding
(whether bogus, constructed or whatever[6]), I think that we are on safer
ground treating these tropes as literary and cultural rather than as
necessarily having purely historical referents. Whatever else it may be,
history is, at the least, literature and narrative.[7] Historical events may
be reflected in such biblical tropes as exodus and exile, but they need
not be. As tropes they need not be exhausted by whatever historical
aspect is assigned to them. Surely even biblical poets are to be allowed
some freedom in the use of language and not to be bound absolutely
to our post-Enlightenment obsessions with history.[8] The main biblical

5.   For further observations on the importance of the notions of 'exile', 'depor-
tation' and 'diaspora' in the Bible see Robert P. Carroll, 'Deportation and
Diasporic Discourses in the Prophetic Literature', in James M. Scott (ed.), *Exile:
Old Testament, Jewish, and Christian Conceptions* (*Journal for the Study of
Judaism,* Supplement Series, 56; Leiden: E.J. Brill, 1997), pp. 63-85.

6.   For a discussion of these terms in relation to biblical historiography see
Robert P. Carroll, 'Madonna of Silences: Clio and the Bible', in L.L. Grabbe (ed.),
Can a 'History of Israel' Be Written? (European Seminar in Historical Methodol-
ogy, 1; JSOTSup, 245; Sheffield: Sheffield Academic Press, 1997), pp. 84-103.

7.   Here the writings of Hayden White may be regarded as *de rigueur*, but I
will assume that each and every member of the Seminar has read White's *oeuvre*
on history as narrative. In particular, see Hayden White, *Metahistory: The
Historical Imagination in Nineteenth-Century Europe* (Baltimore: The Johns Hopkins University Press, 1973); *idem, Tropics of Discourse: Essays in Cultural
Criticism* (Baltimore: The Johns Hopkins University Press, 1978).

8.   This obsession with *the Bible as history* is very much the fruit of post-Enlightenment historical-critical thinking about the Bible: see Hans-Georg Gadamer,
'Supplement I Hermeneutics and Historicism (1965)', in *idem, Truth and Method*

evidence—if *evidence* it be—for thinking in terms of the Babylonian captivity as constituting a well-defined period of exile, that is, as a period of time with a definite beginning and an equally definite ending, comes from the Chronicler and the literature associated with him.[9] Here the notion of a fixed-period exile is constituted by the Chronicler's representation of the deportation coming to an end with the instruction of the Persian emperor Cyrus that the temple in Jerusalem should be rebuilt. Furthermore, the Chronicler's representation of the deportation as a 70-year period during which the land kept sabbath (2 Chron. 36.20-21) gives to the notion of the deportation a greater and sacral significance than it would otherwise have had. Not permanent deportation but temporary exile and then exile as a kind of *prolonged sabbath* for the land are the contributions of the Chronicler to the myth-making factor in the presentation of the Babylonian captivity. This *sabbathization* of the deportation turns it effectively into an exile and produces the concomitant myth of the empty land whereby the Palestinian homeland *emptied* awaits the return of the deportees.[10]

The Chronicler, and the literature associated with the Chronicler (Ezra–Nehemiah), represents the story of Judah as ending in exile, that

(trans. Joel Weinsheimer and Donald G. Marshall; New York: Continuum, 2nd rev. edn, 1995), pp. 505-41, esp. pp. 522-27.

9. For various views of this vexed issue see Peter R. Ackroyd, *Exile and Restoration: A Study of Hebrew Thought of the Sixth Century BC* (OTL; London: SCM Press, 1968); *idem*, 'The History of Israel in the Exilic and Post-exilic Periods', in George W. Anderson (ed.), *Tradition and Interpretation: Essays by Members of the Society for Old Testament Study* (Oxford: Clarendon Press, 1979), pp. 320-50; Joseph Blenkinsopp, *Ezra–Nehemiah: A Commentary* (OTL; London: SCM Press, 1989), on the one hand, and Sara Japhet, *I & II Chronicles: A Commentary* (OTL; London: SCM Press, 1993), and Hugh G.M. Williamson, 'The Composition of Ezra i-vi', *JTS* NS 34 (1983), pp. 1-30, on the other.

10. The notion of an empty land need imply no more than a textual return because there was no actual empty land, so why should there have been an actual return? The Chronicler creates the myth of an empty land in order to facilitate a return of people to repopulate the land. But the land was already populated! On these matters see H.M. Barstad, *The Myth of the Empty Land: A Study in the History and Archaeology of Judah During the 'Exilic' Period* (Symbolae osloenses, 28; Oslo: Scandinavian University Press, 1996); Robert P. Carroll, 'The Myth of the Empty Land', in David Jobling and Tina Pippin (eds.), *Ideological Criticism of Biblical Texts* (Semeia, 59; Atlanta: Scholars Press, 1992), pp. 79-93; *idem*, 'Clio and Canons: In Search of a Cultural Poetics of the Hebrew Bible', *BibInt* 5 (1997), pp. 300-323 (esp. pp. 308-15 on 'The Myth of the Empty Land').

is, in a series of deportations culminating in a return to Palestine. Other biblical literature knows of deportations and, what I would want to call, *permanent exile* or exile without return.[11] Between these different literary representations of the matter there arises the question embodied in the title of this paper: 'Exile! What exile?'. Further questions suggest themselves: How then are we to define this exile? How are we to explain its nature? When did it end? If so many people remained in a state of deportedness, can the exile be said to have ended? What kind of exile is it where the bulk of the people never did return to their own land, but only a token number went back as if those who were left behind did not count at all? One must also ask, what was the relation of those who returned to those who were deported some 70 years previously? Were they the *same* people or their descendants or even different people? What may be *reliably* said about this notion of exile in relation to the reading of biblical texts and in relation to the so-called 'real' world outside of these texts (another big question in its own right!)? Too many questions, I fear. *Questions without end.* Questions without definitive answers too because they are too difficult to be answered from the paucity of information available in the biblical text. But these are the very questions which need to be addressed by this historiography Seminar.

I ask these questions because they have been bothering me for a long time and I wish to use this paper to explore my troubled thoughts about the use of the term 'exile' as a determinative or regulative principle for reading the Hebrew Bible. Various books have been written by members of the Guild of Biblical Studies with titles that include the term 'exile': for example, Enno Janssen's *Juda in der Exilszeit* (1956), Charles Whitley's *The Exilic Age* (1957), Peter Ackroyd's *Exile and Restoration* (1968), Thomas Raitt's *A Theology of Exile* (1977) and Ralph Klein's *Israel in Exile* (1979), to name but five.[12] My sense of disquiet with such titles arises from my point of view that to use the

11. See M.A. Knibb, 'The Exile in the Literature of the Intertestamental Period', *Heythrop Journal* 17 (1976), pp. 253-72; Robert P. Carroll, 'Israel, History of (Post-monarchic period)', *ABD*, III, pp. 567-76.

12. Enno Janssen, *Juda in der Exilszeit: Ein Beitrag zur Frage der Enstehung des Judentums* (FRLANT, 51; Göttingen: Vandenhoeck & Ruprecht, 1956); Charles Whitley, *The Exilic Age* (London: Longmans, Green & Co., 1959); Thomas Raitt, *A Theology of Exile: Judgment/Deliverance in Jeremiah and Ezekiel* (Philadelphia: Fortress Press, 1977); Ralph Klein, *Israel in Exile: A Theological Interpretation* (Philadelphia: Fortress Press, 1979).

term 'exile' in a book title is to connive at, conspire or collaborate with the biblical text in furthering the myth represented by the ideological shaping of biblical history. It is the taking of an ancient Jerusalem-orientated point of view by writers who are twentieth-century scholars as if such a partisan position could be taken up by non-participants without involving considerable bad faith (*mauvaise foi*). The point I am getting around to making is this: from the position of modern readers of the Bible there can really only be a sense of exile as something propounded by a Jerusalem- or Palestinian-orientated point of view. From a Babylonian Jewish community, an Egyptian Jewish community or even a modern reader's point of view, life in the diaspora may not have been seen as exilic at all. It is all a question of point of view and perspective. It is also—and this is as much what my paper is about as anything else—a question of what biblical scholars should be doing when they attempt to state, expound or *re*present the representations of what is thought to be in the Bible. As ever in this postmodern period we are talking about the vexed issue of representation and indeed of the crisis in representation—as well as the fundamentally basic questions about *how* to read texts (whether ancient or modern) and the situatedness of all such readings.

Now of course everybody has to be somewhere and there can be no such thing as *a view from nowhere*, but biblical scholarship is very prone to forget about the situatedness of all readings or indeed of all writings too.[13] To talk about the exile is to take a position following or favouring the Jerusalem-orientated point of view. For those of us who do not live in Jerusalem that is not really an option available for us to be exercising. In the diaspora people may regard themselves as living in a diaspora or they may regard it as home (*Heimat*). For some such people there may be a rhetoric of return or a discourse of exile; or there again there may be no such thing at all. How many generations does it require for a group of people to start thinking of themselves as indigenous, native or aboriginal? For example, black people in the United States currently favour regarding themselves as *Afro*-American, thus highlighting their Africanness and African origins. But it might be a

13. The phrase comes from the title of Thomas Nagel's book, *The View from Nowhere* (Oxford: Oxford University Press, 1989), and refers to the impossibility of anybody taking such a view. Everybody has to be somewhere, so the views we take are always the view from somewhere and not from nowhere. Every (re)reading is a *situated* reading, contextualized by many specific and general factors.

fundamental error to imagine that all such people intend to return to Africa some day or, indeed, to imagine that Africa would welcome or recognize them either. But black people in Britain would want to be recognized as British, while including a sense of their own ethnic origins. Of course for ideological and identity reasons groups may choose not to think of themselves as being original to anywhere in particular, in favour of an ideology of exiledness or a discourse of not-being-at-home-anywhere.[14] Such possibilities apply among many Jewish groups, especially after the European death-camps of this century, but they are options and need not necessarily be applied in any or all situations. Whether diaspora constitutes the inevitable identity marker of being Jewish or some imaginary connection with the imagined land of 'ancient Israel' or of contemporary Israel are issues not easily resolved, even by extended discussion.[15]

This laborious piece of clarification is given in order to emphasize the point that we have little or no discussion of these relativities in the Bible itself, so must invent such a discussion using too few texts to make too many points. Of course no biblical writer would have been a denizen of Jerusalem or Palestine *and also* have lived in Babylonia or Egypt, so we should not expect to read in the Bible a properly relativized account of the matter. *The relativities of the matter are for observers, not for participants.* It is only us moderns who read the Bible who are in a position to observe every point of view without having to hold any specific belief about the matter, even though religious folk may well imagine themselves to be holding a biblical point of view (as if

14. The voluminous writings of George Steiner address some of these issues in relation to Jewish self-consciousness and identity: among so many writings see, e.g., his exemplary 1985 essay, 'Our Homeland, the Text', in George Steiner (ed.), *No Passion Spent: Essays 1978–1996* (London: Faber & Faber, 1995), pp. 304-27. On the construction of national identity see Benedict Anderson, *Imagined Communities: Reflections on the Origin and Spread of Nationalism* (London: Verso, rev. edn, 1991); and Paul Connerton, *How Societies Remember* (Cambridge: Cambridge University Press, 1989).

15. There is a huge literature on the ideology and politics of identity that, while germane to this discussion, space does not permit to be dealt with here. It is also a site of contested interpretations between Jews and Christians as well as between land and diaspora dispositions of social groupings. For a Jewish point of view and discussion see Daniel and Jonathan Boyarin, 'Diaspora: Generation and the Ground of Jewish Identity', *Critical Inquiry* 19 (1993), pp. 693-725 (and the many essays of George Steiner).

selecting one view out of so many in the Bible constituted *the* reading of the text). There are, of course, biblical books that depict Jewish life in the diaspora, where individual Jews or Jewish families are represented as having flourished in the service of the empire and gave no impression of being in a state of constant frenzy about returning to the so-called holy land or holy city. Books such as the diaspora novellas are reflected in the scrolls of Daniel, Tobit, Judith, and so on. Perhaps only Psalm 137 attempts to depict a longing for Jerusalem, a desire for Zion, which is founded on the alienation of living in Babylon. But we have no means of knowing how typical, ideal or idiosyncratic this chauvinistic point of view may have been as represented by this famous psalm. Furthermore, we do not know whether the psalm represents the deportation generation, first-generation diaspora or long-term diaspora points of view. For all we know about the psalm it could have been a paean to Jerusalem written by a member of the temple guild in that city using an imaginary exilic setting for its point of view. When it comes to trying to guess the original *Sitz im Leben* of individual psalms in the book of Psalms all our scholarship is either mere speculation or the parroting of handed down received opinions (à la Russell's epigraphic observation).

Preliminary questions about the nature, endurance and constituencies of the deportation, exile and diaspora periods could be multiplied throughout this paper. At the same time, it must be emphasized that there are many other questions which should be asked about the literature bearing on the topoi of exile, deportation and diaspora. Although it is a truism to say that virtually everything in the Hebrew Bible is problematic from a modern or historical point of view, the literature relating to the diaspora does appear to be especially complex and difficult. Many literary questions have to be resolved satisfactorily (or at least to various scholars' own satisfaction) before one can proceed to make any judgments about or to use the literature itself in relation to historical research of the ancient past. For example, scholars are seriously divided about the relationship between the Chronicler and the Ezra–Nehemiah literature. Did the Chronicler write or edit Ezra–Nehemiah or do Ezra–Nehemiah come from a Chronicler-free environment? In the Ezra–Nehemiah literature there are fundamental problems which have to be sorted out before questions about the historicalness (or even historicity) of the material can be determined. As Hugh Williamson rightly observes:

> It is widely recognized that a satisfactory historical reconstruction of the
> reforms of Ezra and Nehemiah is dependent upon *a resolution of the
> many literary problems* associated with Ezra vii-x and Nehemiah.[16]

If we cannot resolve the many literary problems in this literature, then
the Bible is going to provide rather poor resource material for writing
the history of whichever time we may wish to assign these texts to in
the Persian (or Hellenistic) period. Any concatenation of such problems
must render any and all historiographic approaches to reading the Bible
highly suspect as attempts at historical reconstructions of an imagined
past.

While it is not possible to go into all these questions here, at least one
consequence of this factor is that many scholars are going to disagree
about the interpretation of these problems, so there is not going to
be any agreement among scholars about Ezra–Nehemiah, not to mention the relationship between Chronicles and Ezra–Nehemiah. We are
doomed to be divided by our interpretations on the reading of the biblical literature in relation to the matters of deportation, exile and diaspora. But then what is new about that? On every important interpretative issue involving the Hebrew Bible, biblical scholars are fiercely
divided and in deep disagreement. There is no route that takes us away
from disagreement. The textual data underdetermine any comprehensive interpretation which would have the assent of all biblical scholars.
Not only is that the case, but the data will themselves permit a wide
variety of interpretations around which different scholarly factions can
quarrel *ad infinitum* without any fear of ever arriving at consensus.
Whatever the Guild of Biblical Studies may think to the contrary, the
history and experience of biblical scholarship over the past two centuries is ample testimony to the classical observation: *doctores sunt
scinduntur* (the experts disagree!). At best we can only hope to frag-
ment into factions and clusters of scholars who have agreed to differ
and to support our own distinctive readings of the biblical text in
pursuit of differing reconstructions of the imagined past of the diaspora
communities, especially in relation to the mythic presentation of the
glorious march or the *long trek* back to Jerusalem by the Babylonian
aliyya represented by the account in Ezra 1–3.[17]

16. Williamson, 'Composition', p. 1 (emphasis mine).
17. I am very conscious of writing this piece during the Marching Season in
Northern Ireland (July 1997), so can hardly avoid referring to the trek back from

Questions about the historical reliability of the Ezra–Nehemiah mate-rial—our old friends Bogus History or the Biblical Fact[18]—inevitably keep presenting themselves to this Seminar. There is no escape for his-torians from such questions, even though postmodern textualists may avoid such problems by fondly imagining that 'final form of the text' approaches are the answer to historical-critical matters—an equally problematic approach, but not acknowledged as such by these refusers of history and tradition. Yet if we are going to try to produce a *histori-cal narrative* of the representations of the end of exile and the return to Jerusalem by the deportees based on Ezra 1–3 and Nehemiah 7, it will be necessary to demonstrate the reliability of the information available to us in these chapters. On the other hand, historical reliability may not be so important if we are prepared to accept these biblical narratives on other grounds, perhaps of a literary or aesthetic nature. Recently I was rereading Herodotus's *Histories* and came across the following wise words of Hugh Bowden on the subject of historical reliability in Hero-dotus which might well, *mutatis mutandis*, serve biblical studies:

> There is one question which I have so far avoided: how much of Herodotus' *Histories* is reliable? How much of it is true? This is because I do not think that it is actually a useful question. Rawlinson's footnotes often indicate where something described by Herodotus is known from elsewhere, but much of what is described is impossible to confirm or refute. Internal inconsistencies may indicate that something is wrong, but otherwise we must take the narrative for what it is: Herodotus has recorded what the Greeks and others of his time claimed to be their version of the past; he gives a picture of how they saw their present. Any attempt to give an account of past events is bound to be incomplete, partial, and no doubt in some instances false. It is not simply as a source of information about past history that we should read Herodotus. Far

Babylon to Jerusalem as if it were a Grand March back to Jerusalem 'Orangemen-style'. In spite of the long lists of names given in Ezra 1–3 and Neh. 7 (more than 40,000 people), no details are given of the journey itself nor of the logistics whereby so many people made such a perilous three-month journey through bandit-infested wilderness. The absence of such necessary detail makes the representation of the return from exile analogous to the equally bereft-of-substantive-information representation of the exodus legend in Exod. 1–24.

18. For these terms see my contribution to the Dublin Historiography Seminar (1996), 'Madonna of Silences: Clio and the Bible', pp. 92-93.

more importantly than that, he provides us with a wealth of material whose value greatly exceeds the issue whether everything that he describes happened just as he says it did.[19]

Could we agree to say that questions about the reliability of biblical history, whether as bogus or authentic, are irrelevant because we cannot answer them in the first place? The current dogma of reactionary approaches to the Bible may be summed up in the oft-quoted phrase 'the absence of evidence is not evidence of absence'[20]—but try using this dogma with similarly reactionary New Testament scholars on the sex life of Jesus! It is, of course, an utterly useless piece of dogma because it demonstrates nothing and leaves everything where it was before the slogan was uttered. As Wittgenstein said a long time ago in his Proposition 7: *Wovon man nicht sprechen kann, darüber muss man schweigen* (what we cannot speak about we must pass over in silence).[21] Now I know Willie McKane will accuse me of laziness here, of conveniently not having to do the historical research entailed in biblical scholarship by taking this line.[22] In my own defence I would have to say that it is neither my intention nor my style to avoid doing the work. It is much more the case that there is not really anything to be done here because the connections between the biblical text and the world outside of the text are far too few to be of any consequence and far too problematic to warrant the over-confidence of traditional bibli-

19. Hugh Bowden, 'Introduction', in *idem* (ed.), *Herodotus, the Histories* (trans. George Rawlinson; The Everyman Library; London: J.M. Dent, 1992), p. xxvii. I use Bowden's comments here because I think the question of the historical reliability of Herodotus provides a good parallel for the same question in biblical studies. I would have to admit that while I think Herodotus may have better title to the description 'historian' than the biblical writers have, I am far from certain as to what would be a good or adequate descriptor for the biblical writers (mythopoets? Bardic narrators?).

20. For the source of this phrase see W. Röllig, 'On the Origin of the Phoenicians', *Berytus* 31 (1983), pp. 79-93 (82). Unless we are to reduce biblical scholarship to argument by the exchanging of slogans, it would be better to abandon the naive approach inherent in this particular dogma.

21. Ludwig Wittgenstein, *Tractatus Logico-Philosophicus* (trans. D.F. Pears and B.F. McGuinness; London: Routledge & Kegan Paul, 1996), pp. 150-51.

22. At least that is how I read some of his criticisms of my approach to interpreting the book of Jeremiah in William McKane, *A Critical and Exegetical Commentary on Jeremiah. II. Commentary on Jeremiah XXVI–LII* (ICC; Edinburgh: T. & T. Clark, 1996).

cal scholarship's reading of the text. We have no grid on which we can map the details of the biblical narrative alongside the external data available in order to create a reliable historical picture which would satisfy normal historians (if such things as 'normal historians' can be said to exist).

Each and every biblical scholar will have to say for themselves just what it is in Ezra 1–6 and Nehemiah 7 that they think affords us access to the 'historical story' or what pieces of the text should be utilized in constructing our individual stories of how things were in relation to the return from exile. A somewhat different paper would introduce here a lengthy and exhaustive exposition of the work of Charles Cutler Torrey on this subject, but I shall desist from offering such a paper.[23] If there is a consensus among biblical scholars in this area it seems to take the form of adopting a profoundly anti-Torrey position (cf. Williamson) and the Guild of Biblical Studies is above all things an interpretative community where majority positions dominate the field and these count for what passes as knowledge in the Guild.[24] At the same time as acknowledging this stranglehold position that certain viewpoints within the Guild have tended to have over other points of view, I would like to put in a strong word for Torrey here. To a certain extent—the precise measurement of that extent I shall leave to further debate and reflection—I would want to support Torrey's point of view about the exile:

> In modern Biblical science the Babylonian exile has been given the central place, and made the dominating factor, in both the religious and the literary history of the Hebrews. This conception is, in fact, one of the most characteristic features of the critical theory which in our generation has been elaborated by Wellhausen, Robertson Smith, and their fellows and successors, and is now held by all of the more advanced Old Testament scholars. Straight across the face of Israelite theory is drawn a heavy line, the exile, which is supposed to mark a very abrupt and complete change in almost every sphere of the people's life. Above the

23. See C.C. Torrey, *Ezra Studies* (Chicago: University of Chicago Press, 1910); for further works of Torrey see Ackroyd, *Exile and Restoration*, pp. 21-22.

24. H.G.M. Williamson, *Ezra, Nehemiah* (WBC, 16; Waco, TX: Word Books, 1985), pp. xxviii-xxxii. Much of this position is probably due to the Albrightean domination of the field and it would be my guess that until Albright's ghost is laid Torrey will never come into his own in biblical studies. I have commented elsewhere on this state of affairs (cf. Carroll, 'Torrey, C.C.', in Richard J. Coggins and J. Leslie Houlden (eds.), *A Dictionary of Biblical Interpretation* (London: SCM Press, 1990), p. 697.

line is what is called the 'prophetic' period, and below it the 'legal'
period, the latter being regarded as altogether inferior to the former.
Before the exile, the great writers and preachers of Israel; after it,
inferior teachers and imitators. In the earlier period, a continuous and
admirable development, in national character, literature, and religion; in
the later period, a low level at the start, and a steady decline, in all these
respects. The theory of the exile itself, and of the nature of the
'restoration' after it, is fundamental to these conceptions. According to
the accepted view, the Jews who had been deported to Babylonia
prepared the elaborate ritual code which was to regulate the life of the
new community. And the restored Israel, after the long period of
suspended animation, was a church founded from without, and a community devoting itself henceforth to the study and practice of the new
ceremonial law.[25]

I tend to agree with him that the dominant notion of the exile in biblical
scholarship is 'a thoroughly mistaken theory'.[26] Torrey may have been
writing about how things were at the turn of the last century, but I
would have to say that in my judgment I do not think things have
changed much as we approach the turn of the next century. Some
things may be changing at the moment, but the dominant thesis laid
down by Wellhausen and Robertson Smith still seems to have most
scholars in its thrall. I would hope that the next century of biblical
scholarship will have radically changed from what it was in this
century. This historiography Seminar and the valiant work being done

---

25. Torrey, *Ezra Studies*, pp. 287-88. I would concur with Torrey in his
attribution of the construction of this point of view to Wellhausen and Robertson
Smith. Elsewhere I have criticized Smith's overly *Christianized* reading of the
Hebrew Bible (cf. Carroll, 'The Biblical Prophets as Apologists for the Christian
Religion: Reading William Robertson Smith's *The Prophets of Israel* Today', in
William Johnstone [ed.], *William Robertson Smith: Essays in Reassessment*
[JSOTSup, 189; Sheffield: Sheffield Academic Press, 1994], pp. 148-57), but I do
not wish to develop that critique any further here. I am surprised, however, that
such a normally astute authority as John Emerton regarded the view expressed by
me of Robertson Smith as unusual (Emerton, 'Review of W. Johnstone, *William
Robertson Smith: Essays in Reassessment*', in *VT* 47 (1997), p. 271). I would have
thought that anybody capable of reading a text for its ideological implications
would have seen this aspect of Robertson Smith's work quite clearly—after all,
Charles Torrey did.

26. Torrey, *Ezra Studies*, p. 288.

by the new historians (if not new historicism among biblical scholars) should help effectively to bring such a desired change about.[27]

Torrey's viewpoint that 'We have no trustworthy evidence that any numerous company returned from Babylonia, nor is it intrinsically likely that such a return took place' is germane to the discussion here.[28] Of course scholars may dissent from this point of view and assert that the narratives of Ezra 1–6, Nehemiah 7 represent solid, reliable history and therefore they constitute a genuine witness to a mass return from exile. Personally I have great difficulty with any such understanding of Ezra–Nehemiah for many, many reasons, including the difficulty of accounting for all the literature that knows of no such return (e.g. so much of the biblical and extra-biblical literature, including the Qumran Scrolls). The amount of textual corruption in the lists of returning exiles in Ezra and Nehemiah is significant (see Williamson, 'Composition'), whatever our view of the dependency of Ezra on Nehemiah, and needs to be factored into any account we may care to construct of the period. Whether we follow Garbini in regarding Ezra as a late invention of a much later period or prefer to insist on *some* degree of 'historicity' (however defined or left unmeasured) for such a scribal figure and whatever the order and number of comings and goings of Ezra and Nehemiah, everywhere we look there are insuperable obstacles to being confident of the historical reliability of Ezra (either as book or as person).[29] It seems to me that unless we impose theological dogmas on the text at some point in our discussions, a (high) degree of scepticism is warranted when we read Ezra for reliable historical information.[30]

27. For discussion of this new historiography (or new historicism) in contemporary biblical studies see Robert P. Carroll, 'Clio and Canons: In Search of a Cultural Poetics of the Hebrew Bible', in Stephen D. Moore (ed.), *The New Historicism*, *BibInt* 5 (1997), pp. 300-23 (all the essays in this special edition of *Biblical Interpretation* are of relevance here); *Carroll*, 'Poststructuralist Approaches: New Historicism and Postmodernism', in John Barton (ed.), *The Cambridge Companion to Biblical Interpretation* (Cambridge: Cambridge University Press, 1998), pp. 50-66.

28. Torrey, *Ezra Studies*, p. 288.

29. On Ezra see G. Garbini, *History and Ideology in Ancient Israel* (trans. John Bowden; London: SCM Press, 1988), pp. 151-69.

30. This is one of the current imponderables in the Guild: so many biblical scholars are theologians and/or professional cult figures in various branches of the Christian churches, yet never give any indication of such commitments in their writings. So it is always difficult to know to what extent their religious beliefs and

While these points could be developed considerably here I do not wish to do so because I want to move on to some other points which also bear on the issue to hand.

Let us suppose, just for the sake of argument, that a large, 40 something thousand, strong mass of people did leave Babylonia on the *great trek* to Jerusalem, numerous questions still remain to be asked and to be answered. Would such an event have been the end of the exile or just an end for some of the exiles? Suppose many more people had remained behind in the diaspora than had returned, would such a state of affairs have constituted the *ending* of the exile? Surely that cannot have been the case. If *more* people remained in Babylonia and elsewhere in the diaspora than (ever) returned to Jerusalem and/or Palestine, then surely the exile (deportation) could not be deemed to have come to an end? In other words, the most obvious question poses itself: did the exile ever end? If it is deemed to have come to an end, then when would that have been? In further other words, if lots of people went on living in the diaspora and their descendants stayed there for thousands of years (until final flight or massacre in the twentieth century), then in what sense can the exile ever be said to have come to an end? What *kind* of an exile is it that has both a piecemeal or occasional end and a continuous existence through thousands of years? I think we need to change our language, to rethink our nomenclature for describing the period and to clarify our concepts at this point in the discussion.

Can biblical scholarship ever be satisfied with the standard compromise of 'Yes' and 'No'? On the one hand, to the question 'did the exile ever end?', we may answer: 'Yes, when all those people in Ezra 1–3 and Nehemiah 7 returned to Jerusalem and the homeland.' At the least perhaps such an event may be treated as a *symbolic* ending of exile, that is, as a kind of *pars pro toto* ending of the deportation? On the other

dogmas drive (or are driven by) their scholarship. What is even more curious is that frequently these issues are never raised at all in the doing of biblical scholarship, as if they had absolutely no bearing on the what or how of reading the Bible! See Iain W. Provan, 'Ideologies, Literary and Critical: Reflections on Recent Writing on the History of Israel', *JBL* 114 (1995), pp. 585-606, for a notable instance of this strange practice wherein the writer conceals his own ideological commitments while condemning those with whom he disagrees as if neutrality should be extended only to himself as arbiter of taste, judgment and correct belief (dogma), so that one is led to wonder whether such non-disclosure is significant. Or should it be thought of as concealment? Who can tell! Go, figure.

hand, to the (same) question 'did the exile ever end?', the answer will be: 'No, it is still going on.' In fact, *the diaspora has turned out to be the most dominant feature of Judaism* over the past millennium and a half of orthodox Jewish existence. *It is the dispersion itself that is the central feature and key to understanding Jewish history.* Here we may need to abandon using the language of 'exile' or modify considerably our usage of such language. I think Torrey is right with his emphasis on the dissolution of the nation, its dispersion, as 'a calamity which was far more significant, and whose mark on the heart of Israel was much deeper'.[31] Contrary to the views of Wellhausen, Robertson Smith and countless other Christian apologist scholars, the diaspora was the turning-point which gave rise to the superior post-catastrophe communities after the death of the nation:

> But the scattering of Israel to the four corners of the earth meant the death of the nation, and only the miracle of a second 'return from Egypt' (Is. 43.16ff., 48.21, etc.) could restore the dead to life. The people were, indeed, 'purified in the furnace of affliction,' and were spiritually the better for it, after they had once risen to their feet again. What their religious life suffered in the years immediately following 586 was merely the temporary arresting of a continuous and splendid development. They were not crushed to the point of despair, not driven into any such selfish exclusiveness as is pictured in the Chronicler's imaginary history. The prophets and (still more) the Psalms teach us better than that. The destruction of the temple was the turning-point, partly for evil, but more for good, seeing that the nation as a political entity was doomed in any case. At all events, it was this catastrophe, not the exile, which constituted the dividing line between the two eras. The terms 'exilic,' 'pre-exilic,' and 'post-exilic' ought to be banished forever from usage, for they are merely misleading, and correspond to nothing that is real in Hebrew literature and life.[32]

I would like to write in bold capitals that last sentence of Torrey's and have it emblazoned on all biblical history textbooks from now on. I say that because I think it is high time that we developed this line of approach to reading the Bible. I know that quite a number of biblical scholars already do refuse to use the ideologically contaminated term 'exile', with its pre- and post-markers. I would just like to hope that many other scholars will in due course come to pursue the same line of refusal to use the conventional nomenclature and develop better ways

31. Torrey, *Ezra Studies*, p. 289.
32. Torrey, *Ezra Studies*, p. 289.

of redescribing and reconfiguring the biblical deportation and diaspora discourses.

In order to conclude this draft of my paper for the historiography Seminar, let me sum up what I think I am arguing for in this paper. If we were to think of the Babylonian onslaught against the Jerusalem centre, temple and whatever, as part of a series of deportations which changed the shape of the communities living around that centre, mainly in terms of decentring the cult in Jerusalem and refocusing on communities in dispersal, Babylonia, Egypt and other parts of the ancient world then become, with time, the great centres of developing Jewish consciousness. The temple guild in Jerusalem will have emerged many centuries after the Babylonian onslaught, but in its ideological literature (what we know as part of the Hebrew Bible), a very different account is given of the matter. The prophetic literature retains (maintains) a very strong awareness of the diaspora, but its tropes seem to be edited into the service of a Jerusalem-centred ideology. Of course this need only be *centre and periphery discourse* that reflects Jerusalem-based traditions. In the diaspora very different traditions may have played their part in maintaining identity and cultural propserity. The very many references in the prophetic literature to the ingathering of the dispersed communities (e.g. Isa. 60.1-14; Jer. 31.2-14; Ezek. 36.16-38; also the slogan-type phrase *šûb šebût*[33]) may reflect a genuine expectation for the restoration of the diaspora or they may simply reflect the *pious rhetoric* of 'next-year-in-Jerusalem' type of discourse. From this distance in time it is impossible to say how the many references to the diaspora embedded in the prophets should be read historically. Perhaps we should read them as fantasy, as piety, as genuine aspiration or expectation, as ideology or as the flattering rhetoric that was designed to maintain Jerusalem's self-image of being the centre in contrast to the peripheries of the diaspora. Who can tell how they should be read? Indeed, who is to say that there is only one way of reading such protean rhetoric? All I think I would want to say about the rhetoric of dispersion and ingathering so common in the prophets is that it certainly represents an awareness in these scrolls of the post-586 catastrophe and

---

33. On the sense of this cliché in the Bible see John M. Bracke, 'שׁוּב שְׁבוּת: A Reappraisal', *ZAW* 97 (1985:), pp. 233-44.

of life lived within the larger context of the diaspora.[34] Thus I come back to where I began this paper: the Hebrew Bible is a literature of dispersal and deportation, of representations of and reflections on life lived outside one centre and inside other centres (centre and periphery are relativized by perspective). There is more than one centre in the Hebrew Bible, though the tendency of the 'canonical' text is for the Jerusalem writers to have contaminated all the other writings with their own ideological holdings and values. No wonder among the prime requisites for any reading of the Hebrew Bible is the need for a strong application of *Ideologiekritik* (ideological criticism) in order to overcome the ideological biases which the writers may have incorporated into the biblical text.[35]

34. See further comments on these matters in Carroll, 'Deportation and Diasporic Discourses in the Prophetic Literature', pp. 66-82.

35. This is the point where my paper originally ended, but after the news of the sudden death of Ferdinand Deist on 12 July 1997 I would want to emphasize further the importance of an *Ideologiekritik* approach to reading the Bible. Ferdinand was a great champion of the *Ideologiekritik* approach to the Bible and taught me so much about it. I am proud to have had him as a friend who carried on a marvellous correspondence with me during the dark years of apartheid and to have got to know him personally after the demise of apartheid. His loss, a loss which I still feel keenly as I rewrite this paper (December 1997), originally given in Lausanne (July 1997), puts me at a loss for words.

'THE EXILE' UNDER THE THEODOLITE:
HISTORIOGRAPHY AS TRIANGULATION

Lester L. Grabbe

The entity of 'the exile' is not easy to come to grips with. In one sense, we have a lot of material to work with, both in the Old Testament where the concept was significant, and in modern scholarly writings. Yet if there is one period where much so easily slips from one's grasp when the question of history is introduced, it is probably 'the exile', perhaps only exceeded by the 'patriarchal period'. The exile is a powerful symbol. It is this very fact that makes it more difficult to come to grips with from a historical perspective.[1]

The exile is also unusual in that we have little that claims to be a description of the exile. We have a detailed account of the events preceding the fall of Samaria and Jerusalem in 2 Kings and 2 Chronicles; similarly, the first few chapters of Ezra tell about the return and reconstruction of the city and country. But even though a book such as Lamentations claims to be a response to the fall of Jerusalem, no writing ostensibly describes the transport of peoples to Babylonia or what happened to them once they got there. Apart from a few brief references in Ezekiel to the Jews taken to Babylonia in 597 BCE, and in Jeremiah to events in Judah immediately following the fall of Jerusalem, the exile is a blank. If we are to get at it, we must do what surveyors do: we must take bearings from several angles and then

---

1. One is reminded of John Bright's statement about Moses, 'To deny that role [in the founding of the Israelite religion] to Moses would force us to posit another person of the same name!' (*A History of Israel* [Philadelphia: Westminster Press; London: SCM Press, 3rd edn, 1980], p. 127). But necessity is the mother of invention! To me, his statement leads to the opposite conclusion than he reached: if the situation seemed to call for a Moses, then one may have been invented to fill the need. In the same way, if the exile has been so useful in the literature and theology, it could have been invented to fill a need.

extrapolate by agreed principles to results which cannot be directly confirmed but can be reasonably inferred. In the same way, just as builders insert a triangle into their structure to give it solidity, the coincidence of unrelated data may give support to an event that is not directly attested.

Of the many possible topics which could be dealt with here—since 'the exile' is, after all, a big subject—I propose to look at three issues. First, I shall ask the question of whether exiled communities lost their identity and whether they ever returned to their native lands. If the Jewish return appears unique in history, that might make us question the historicity of the incident. Secondly, I want to consider what can be confirmed from external sources about the events described in the biblical text. Finally, it will be useful to look at what the history that emerges from this study, if any, looks like.

Exiled Communities: Identity and Return

This section asks two questions: (1) did exiled communities maintain their identity; and (2) did they ever return to their homeland? These two questions are quite important for evaluating the biblical accounts of a community of returned exiles from the Babylonian captivity. Although one should be careful of treating the matter as one of genetic identity, the question of ethnic or national identity is an important one, and the loss of such identity by the exiled communities is significant for any study.

On the question of loss of identity, there are many examples supporting both the loss of identity and the retention of it. The Assyrians tended to exile people as families and communities rather than just scattered individuals.[2] This could make it easier for people to retain their old identity. That some people did maintain an ethnic, geographical or national identity is very clear from many inscriptions which identify individuals by such labels. The references to individuals

---

2.   Bustenay Oded, *Mass Deportations and Deportees in the Neo-Assyrian Empire* (Wiesbaden: Reichert, 1979), pp. 22-25. See also Oded's article 'Observations on the Israelite/Judaean Exiles in Mesopotamia during the Eighth–Sixth Centuries BCE', in K. van Lerberghe and A. Schoors (eds.), *Immigration and Emigration within the Ancient Near East* (Festchrift E. Lipinski; Orientalia lovaniensia analecta, 65; Leuven: Peeters/Departement Orientalistiek, 1995), pp. 205-12.

as 'Sidonian', 'Tyrian', 'Egyptian', 'Samarian' and the like would be meaningless if they had no connection with place of origin or maintenance of ethnic identity.[3]

Yet we know that people did evidently assimilate, at least over a long period of time. The prime example is the Israelites from the Northern Kingdom. There are references to Samarians over the decades after the fall of Samaria in 722 BCE.[4] During the Neo-Babylonian, Persian and Greek periods they cease to be mentioned in the Mesopotamian sources. A memory of the 'ten tribes' is kept alive in Jewish sources, but it is not clear that this is based on actual knowledge of the continued existence of the exiled northern tribes. It seems more likely that the inspiration comes from the biblical literature and the memory that Israel was exiled and had not returned.[5]

We also know of communities that maintained their identity over long periods of time. A Tyrian settlement in Nippur maintained itself 150 years after Nebuchadnezzar brought prisoners from Tyre.[6] Perhaps

3.   See the many references in Oded, *Mass Deportations, passim*. Also Israel Eph'al, 'The Western Minorities in Babylonia in the 6th–5th Centuries BC: Maintenance and Cohesion', *Or* 47 (1978), pp. 74-90; '"The Samarian(s)" in the Assyrian Sources', in Mordechai Cogan and Israel Eph'al (eds.), *Ah, Assyria...Studies in Assyrian History and Ancient Near Eastern Historiography Presented to Hayim Tadmor* (Scripta Hierosolymitana, 33; Jerusalem: Magnes Press, 1991), pp. 36-45; Ran Zadok, 'Phoenicians, Philistines, and Moabites in Mesopotamia', *BASOR* 230 (1978), pp. 57-65; Zadok, 'On Some Foreign Population Groups in First-Millennium Babylonia', *Tel Aviv* 6 (1979), pp. 164-81; Zadok, 'Arabians in Mesopotamia during the Late-Assyrian, Chaldean, Achaemenian and Hellenistic Periods Chiefly According to the Cuneiform Sources', *ZDMG* 131 (1981), pp. 42-84; A.C.V.M. Bongenaar and B.J.J. Haring, 'Egyptians in Neo-Babylonian Sippar', *JCS* 46 (1994), pp. 47-58.

4.   See Eph'al, ' "The Samarian(s)" in the Assyrian Sources'. He argues that the further removed in time from the fall of Samaria, the more likely the reference is to non-Israelite inhabitants (or former inhabitants) of the Assyrian province.

5.   Josephus claims that at the time of the siege of Jerusalem by the Romans, some expected that their 'fellow-countrymen beyond the Euphrates' would come to join them (*War* 1.2 §5; cf. 6.6.2 §343). In *Ant.* 11.5.2 §133 he refers to the 'ten tribes beyond the Euphrates', with two tribes in Asia and Europe. *4 Ezra* (2 Esdras) 13.39-47 prophesies the return to Zion of the 'ten tribes' taken captivity beyond the Euphrates. Philo also mentions that many Jews lived beyond the Euphrates, in Babylonia and elsewhere, though he says nothing about the 'ten tribes' (e.g. *Leg. Gai.* 216, 282).

6.   Zadok, 'Phoenicians, Philistines, and Moabites in Mesopotamia', pp. 60, 62.

another good example of this is the Greek settlement of the Branchidae in Sogdiana which originated under Xerxes when they were brought by him from Miletus.[7] When Alexander came across them in the process of his conquest, he found that the inhabitants still spoke Greek and the community maintained its identity, much as many ethnic communities still do today. If the claims in Ezra 4.2 and 4.9-10 about groups brought to Palestine by Assyrian kings are correct, this shows a memory extending over 150 years.[8]

There are not many attested examples of exiled communities which returned to their original habitation, but there are some. For example, rebellious Babylonians were subjected to servitude but then allowed to return to their city by Esarhaddon:

> I summoned all of my artisans and the people of Karduniash (Babylonia) in their totality. I made them carry the basket and laid the headpad upon them... Esagila, the temple of the gods, together with its shrines, Babylon the city under feudal protection...its wall ...its outerwall, from their foundations to their turrets, I built anew, I enlarged, I raised aloft, I made magnificent. The images of the great gods I restored and had them replaced in their shrines to adorn them forever... The sons of Babylon who had been brought to servitude, who had been apportioned to the yoke and the fetter, I gathered together and accounted them for Babylonians. Their citizenship I established anew.[9]

Sennacherib also apparently granted the Phrygian leader Mita the return of some of his people who had been deported, though the facts of the case are somewhat obscure.[10]

---

7. Quintus Curtius 7.5.28-43 (LCL, II, pp. 170-73). Because they had cooperated with the Persians and violated a temple before emigrating, Quintus Curtius claims that Alexander regarded the community as traitorous and slaughtered the city; however, Arrian is silent on the whole episode. Diodorus Siculus apparently once had an account of the incident, according to an ancient table of contents, but a section has been lost from Diodorus's text at this point.

8. As discussed below, though, it is difficult to evaluate these passages because they so well suit the polemical intent of the author.

9. Translation from Daniel David Luckenbill, *Ancient Records of Assyria and Babylonia. II. Historical Records of Assyria from Sargon to the End* (1926–27; repr. London: Histories and Mysteries of Man, 1989), p. 244 (§646). Luckenbill is cited hereafter as *ARAB*.

10. So Oded, *Mass Deportations*, pp. 63, 79. For the text, see H.W.F. Saggs, 'Nimrud Letters, 1952–Part IV; The Urartian Frontier', *Iraq* 20 (1958), pp. 182-212, especially Letter 39 (ND 2759), though Saggs notes that these may be desert-

The questions asked at the beginning of this section can therefore be answered as follows: (1) Communities might lose their identity with time, as seems to have happened with the exiled Samarians; on the other hand, they might maintain identity and even language over a matter of centuries. We have to conclude that one cannot generalize, and whether identity was lost or not has to be addressed in each individual case. (2) Some examples of the return of exiles to their home territory is attested in Assyrian sources. The examples are few, though this could in part be due to the happenstance of recording such incidents or to the episodic nature of the preservation of sources. More returns from exile could have taken place than those known, though it seems unlikely that a large number occurred. But they did sometimes happen, and the alleged return of Jews from exile to form the *gôlā* community in Judah is not unprecedented.

The Biblical Account and External Sources

Only an outline is given here rather than the detailed examination of original sources ultimately needed for a proper full account. The purpose is illustrative rather than definitive and is meant simply to aid the asking and answering of questions about historical methodology.

The Events Leading up to the Fall of Samaria[11]

Biblical Accounts	Contemporary Sources
2 Kgs 15.29; 16.5-9: Rezin of Damascus and Pekah of Israel attack Ahaz of Judah (cf. Isaiah 7). Tiglath-pileser kills Rezin and exiles Damascus.	Tiglath-pileser III takes Damascus (whether he killed Rezin is not preserved).[12]

ers (p. 202); J.N. Postgate, 'Assyrian Texts and Fragments', *Iraq* 35 (1973), pp. 13-36. Cf. also J.D. Hawkings, 'Mita', *RlA* 8.3-4 (1994), pp. 271-73. (Oded's reference [p. 63 n. 162] seems to be incorrect.)

11. On this period in general, see the recent treatment by Bob Becking, *The Fall of Samaria: An Historical and Archaeological Study* (Studies in the History of the Ancient Near East, 2; Leiden: E.J. Brill, 1992).

12. Hayim Tadmor, *The Inscriptions of Tiglath-pileser III King of Assyria: Critical Edition, with Introductions, Translations and Commentary* (Jerusalem:

2 Chron. 28.20: Tilgath-pilne'eser [sic] comes against Ahaz.	Ahaz pays tribute to Tiglath-pileser III.[13]
2 Kgs 15.29: Tiglath-pileser annexes Gilead, Galilee—all the land of Naphtali.	Tiglath-pileser annexes sections of Israel (*Bït-Ḫu-um-ri-a*).[14]
2 Kgs 15.30: Hoshea conspires against Pekah and overthrows him to become king.	Tiglath-pileser kills Pekah, and installs Hoshea.[15]
2 Kgs 17.1-6: Hoshea rebels and is deposed; Shalmaneser of Assyria besieges Samaria and exiles the Israelites. Peoples from Mesopotamia are brought in and settled.	Shalmaneser V destroys Samaria.[16] Sargon II conquers Samaria and exiles 27,000 of its inhabitants.[17] Others are brought in to replace them.[18]

The sources for the period leading up to the capture of Samaria and the 'exile' of the Northern Kingdom are relatively abundant, mainly in the inscriptions of Tiglath-pileser III, the *Babylonian Chronicles* and the inscriptions of Sargon II. This means that the events inside Israel are often reflected in some way in the Assyrian sources, though this may be indirect rather than direct.

The so-called Syro-Ephraimite War is an event affecting the kingdoms of Damascus, Israel and Judah.[19] This is known mainly from

Israel Academy of Sciences and Humanities, 1994), p. 138 (*Summary Inscription 4, 7'-8'*), p. 186 (*Summary Inscription 9, reverse 3-4*).

13. Tadmor, *Tiglath-pileser*, p. 170 (*Summary Inscription 7, 7'-13'*).

14. Tadmor, *Tiglath-pileser*, p. 138 (*Summary Inscriptions 4, 4'-7'*).

15. Tadmor, *Tiglath-pileser*, p. 140 (*Summary Inscription 4, 15'-19'*), p. 188 (*Summary Inscription 9, 9-11*).

16. A.K. Grayson, *Assyrian and Babylonian Chronicles* (Texts from Cuneiform Sources, 5; Locust Valley, NY: J.J. Augustin, 1975), p. 73.

17. *ANET*, pp. 284-85.

18. As noted by Oded (*Mass Deportations*, p. 70) there are no clear statements in Assyrian records about the deportion to the Halah region. One Assyrian reference is unspecific about who was brought in (*ANET*, p. 284; *ARAB*, II, p. 2 [§4]). Another states that defeated Arab tribes were settled there (*ANET*, p. 286; *ARAB*, II, p. 7 [§17]; p. 61 [§118]).

19. A enormous amount of literature has been written on this. In addition to the standard histories of Israel, see most recently Roger Tomes, 'The Reason for the Syro-Ephraimite War', *JSOT* 59 (1993), pp. 55-71.

biblical sources, though it is reflected not only in the narrative of 2 Kings (the main account) but also very briefly in 2 Chronicles, Isaiah 7, and possibly some other passages in the prophetic literature. Without the biblical accounts we would probably not know of such an event, yet the sporadic references in the inscriptions of Tiglath-pileser III provide confirmation of some of the events and do not contradict the basic story. It requires no great courage or rashness to accept the general account found in 2 Kings 15–16. Whether Isaiah actually prophesied to Ahaz about the matter is much harder to know; it is not improbable (since prophets seem to have been a part of Israelite society[20]) but demonstrating the accuracy of Isaiah 7 is impossible at this point.

The same judgment applies to the siege and capture of Samaria and deportation of many Israelites. We know this happened and when, from the Mesopotamian sources, though the precise sequence of events is still uncertain. For example, what part did Shalmaneser V play and what hand did Sargon II have in the matter? It seems likely that the account in 2 Kings is correct that this siege and capture of the city took place in the time of Shalmaneser, but he seems to have died about the time the city fell. Sargon appears to have taken credit for capturing the city; on the other hand, the deportations probably took place during his reign. Also, some sort of revolt in which Samaria was involved evidently occurred in Sargon's second year, and he could rightly claim to have put it down and punished the rebels.[21]

The part of the biblical account in 2 Kings 17 that is not confirmed is the geography of the transport of peoples to and from Samaria. We have no way of knowing whether the Israelites were really taken to the places alleged in 2 Kgs 17.6, nor of whether peoples from the places listed in 2 Kgs 17.24 were actually brought in, though the account is plausible in the light of general Assyrian polices and practices of deportation.[22]

20. See Ch. 4 of my *Priests, Prophets, Diviners, Sages: A Socio-historical Study of Religious Specialists in Ancient Israel* (Valley Forge, PA: Trinity Press International, 1995).

21. For a discussion of the question, see Hayim Tadmor, 'The Campaigns of Sargon II of Assur: A Chronological-Historical Study', *JCS* 12 (1958), pp. 22-40, 77-100, specifically pp. 33-40.

22. Oded, *Mass Deportations*, pp. 69-71; Mordechai Cogan and Hayim Tadmor, *II Kings: A New Translation with Introduction and Commentary* (AB, 11; New York: Doubleday, 1988), pp. 197, 209-10. Becking has looked at the prima facie evidence that the deportations to and from Samaria took place (*Fall of*

The Events Leading up to the Fall of Jerusalem

2 Kgs 23.29: Pharaoh Necho marches to the Euphrates to meet the Assyrians[23] and Josiah is slain.	Egyptians, allied with the Assyrians, attack the Babylonians who are in control of Haran on the Euphrates.[24] Josiah not mentioned in any of extant sources.
Jer. 46.2: Pharaoh Necho defeated at Carchemish by Nebuchadnezzar in the fourth year of Jehoiakim (which was first year of Nebuchadnezzar: Jer. 25.1).	Crown prince Nebuchadnezzar defeats the Egyptians at Carchemish but his further campaigning in Syria is cut short with news of his father's death.[25]
2 Kgs 24.1-7: Jehoiakim becomes Nebuchadnezzar's vassel for three years, then rebels. He is harassed by the Chaldaeans, Aramaeans, Moabites, and Ammonites. 2 Chron. 36.5-7: Jehoiakim is taken captive to Babylon with the temple vessels.[26] Jer. 22.18-19: Jehoiakim's body to be exposed outside the walls of Jerusalem. Dan. 1.1-2: Nebuchanezzar takes Jehoiakim captive in the third year of the latter's reign.	Nebuchadnezzar makes campaigns in the west in his first, second, third and fourth years. In the fourth year the Babylonians and Egyptians fight a stand-off battle which prevents any campaigns in Nebuchadnezzar's fifth year.[27] Nebuchadnezzar attacks the Arabs in the west in his sixth year.
2 Kgs 24.8-16: Nebuchadnezzar takes Jehoiachin captive after a three-month reign, removes 8000 captives and appoints Zedekiah king (cf. also Jer. 24.1; 29.1-2).	In the seventh year he captures the 'city of Judah', seizes its king, appoints a new king and takes tribute.[28]

Samaria, pp. 61-104). However, the only attested deportation to Samaria is of defeated Arab tribes (see n. 18 above).

    23. The Hebrew text is ambiguous and could be 'marched against', but 'marched to' in the sense of joining is a legitimate translation and is likely to be the intent of the writer.

    24. The fate of Jehoiakim in 2 Chron. 36.9-10 is thus alleged to be the same as that of Jehoiachin.

    25. *Chronicle* 3, 59-64 (= Grayson, *Chronicles*, p. 95).

    26. *Babylonian Chronicle* 5, obverse 1-14 (= Grayson, *Chronicles*, pp. 99-100).

    27. *Chronicle* 5, obverse 15 to reverse 7 (= Grayson, *Chronicles*, pp. 100-101).

    28. *Chronicle* 5, reverse 9-13 (Grayson, *Chronicles*, pp. 101-102).

Jer. 37.11-12: Nebuchadnezzar temporarily lifted the siege on Jerusalem because of the Egyptians.	Psammeticus II made a grand tour of Palestine and Syria in 591 BCE, suggesting control of Palestine. He was succeeded in 589 by the vigorous Hophra (Apries).[29]
Jer. 34.6-7: only Lachish and Azekah left of the fortified towns.	The Lachish letters show a certain commander travelling to Egypt (to negotiate before hostilities had begun?), and another suggests Lachish is holding out against the Babylonians even though Azekah may have fallen.[30]
2 Kings 25: Zedekiah rebels in his eleventh year. Jerusalem is besieged and taken by Nebuchadnezzar and many of the people taken captive.	(The *Babylonian Chronicles* cease for Nebuchadnezzar's reign about 594 BCE. No record of the fall of Jerusalem is found in Mesopotamian inscriptions.)

There is a clear differentiation of sources here. Even without taking account of the likely late dating of Daniel, we can still eliminate Dan. 1.1-2 straight away as having a derivative account, most likely based on a misreading of the narrative in 2 Kings and 2 Chronicles.[31] 2 Chronicles does not have a lot relating to events outside Judah proper,

29. See K.S. Freedy and D.B. Redford, 'The Dates in Ezekiel in Relation to Biblical, Babylonian and Egyptian Sources', *JAOS* 90 (1970), pp. 462-85, esp. pp. 478-82; unfortunately, Psammeticus's papyrus makes no reference to Judah. For the text and translation, see F.Ll. Griffith, *Catalogue of the Demotic Papyri in the John Rylands Library, Manchester with Facsimiles and Complete Translations* (3 vols.; Manchester: Manchester University Press, 1909), II, pl. 31-33; III, pp. 92-98.

30. *TSSI*, I, pp. 32-40 (nn. 3-4); *KAI*, nn. 193-94.

31. Despite the efforts of some to redeem Daniel's statement as an actual event (cf. my article 'Fundamentalism and Scholarship: The Case of Daniel', in B.P. Thompson [ed.], *Scripture: Method and Meaning. Essays Presented to Anthony Tyrrell Hanson for his Seventieth Birthday* [Hull: Hull University Press, 1987], pp. 133-52, esp. pp. 138-40), there is no evidence of a siege of Jerusalem by the Babylonians at the time Jehoiakim was reigning. Jehoiakim rebelled after three years according to 2 Kgs 24.1 (though during the *seventh* year of his reign), but the Babylonian response did not come until after his death because of the time it took for Nebuchadnezzar to recover from his defeat. By the time Nebuchadnezzar's army reached Jerusalem, his son Jehoiachin was on the throne, but he quickly capitulated. The author of Daniel has simply confused the accounts in 2 Kgs and 2 Chron.

but its account is mixed. Its assertion that Jehoiakim was taken captive to Babylon looks simply like a repetition of what happened to Jehoiachin. Its account of Jehoiachin is accurate though possibly derivative.[32]

The author of Jeremiah presents an intriguing picture. Much of the text on the siege and fall of Jerusalem (e.g. Jeremiah 39) could have come from 2 Kings. On the other hand, the author of Jeremiah had some accurate data about Nebuchadnezzar's reign which are not found elsewhere in the biblical text. Whether Jeremiah and Zedekiah said and did all they are alleged to have said and done according to the book of Jeremiah is open to question. But Zedekiah's politicking with his advisors, negotiations with Egypt, and vacillation about his relationship with Nebuchadnezzar are plausible in outline form. Even the passing statement that during the siege of Jerusalem Nebuchadnezzar temporarily withdrew his forces because of the Egyptians (Jer. 37.11-12) is supported indirectly from what is known about the Egyptian situation in that period. And yet Jeremiah makes a prediction about Jehoiakim that does not fit any of the data known about his reign (Jer. 22.18-19).[33]

The most impressive source is 2 Kings. Although it has a good deal of detail about events in Judah that have no parallel elsewhere, its picture gets surprising confirmation from incidental points in the Mesopotamian sources. For example, the biblical account gives no reason for the rebellion of Jehoiakim, but its dating and likely cause fit very well with events in Nebuchadnezzar's reign.[34] The capitulation of

---

32. 2 Kgs is normally assumed to be the source of 2 Chron., though this view has recently been challenged by A. Graeme Auld, *Kings Without Privilege: David and Moses in the Story of the Bible's Kings* (Edinburgh: T. & T. Clark, 1994).

33. See the survey in Donald B. Redford, *Egypt, Canaan, and Israel in Ancient Times* (Princeton, NJ: Princeton University Press, 1992), pp. 447-69, who shows that many passages of Jeremiah show a knowledge of the actual historical situation. Although Redford is not normally noted for his defence of the biblical text, here he seems to assume that many of Jeremiah's prophecies are also contemporary with the events described. On the other hand, the problematic nature of much of Jeremiah has been demonstrated by Robert P. Carroll, *From Chaos to Covenant: Uses of Prophecy in the Book of Jeremiah* (London: SCM Press, 1981); *idem*, *Jeremiah: A Commentary* (OTL; London: SCM Press, 1986).

34. Jehoiakim rebelled against Nebuchadnezzar in the very year in which the latter suffered from a devastating encounter with the Egyptians. Because of his losses Nebuchadnezzar did not take to the field the next year. See n. 27 above.

Jerusalem and captivity of Jehoiachin are found in the *Babylonian Chronicles* and also attested in a cuneiform tablet from Babylon.[35]

Compared to some periods in ancient Near Eastern history, we have a good deal of information for the period leading up to the fall of Jerusalem in 587–586 BCE. Information relating specifically to Judah and Jerusalem stops about 594 BCE, apart from the biblical text, but in the preceding two decades a number of sources mention the situation in Judah specifically as well as the events taking place in Mesopotamia and Syria and the west in general. This gives us a considerable degree of confidence in the account in 2 Kings 25 which describes the reign of Zedekiah and the fall of Jerusalem. Jerusalem fell about 587–586 BCE and some of the surviving inhabitants of Jerusalem and Judah were taken captive. The numbers vary somewhat in the sources, though within reasonable limits, and seem plausible.

The Situation in Exile
The problem we have about the Israelites/Jews in exile is that little in the way of contemporary documentation survives until late in the Second Temple period.[36] By that time, one can talk of 'diaspora' but 'exile' is a dubious term.[37] Several writings ostensibly describe Jews and/or the Jewish community in exile during the Persian period or earlier: Esther, Daniel and Tobit (and possibly Deutero–Isaiah, as discussed in the next section). Esther is often dated to the Persian

35. These contain a list of rations distributed to 'Jehoiachin of Judah' and 'the five sons of the king of Judah'; see Ernst F. Weidner, 'Jojachin, König von Juda in babylonischen Keilinschriften', in *Mélanges Syriens offerts à Monsieur René Dussaud* (2 vols.; Paris: J. Gabalda, 1939), II, pp. 923-35.

36. A very useful survey is provided by M.A. Knibb, 'The Exile in the Literature of the Intertestamental Period', *Heythrop Journal* 17 (1976), pp. 253-72.

37. The Elephantine papyri give an insight into a Jewish military colony in upper Egypt in the Persian period, but it can hardly be called an exiled community. The basic account of the community is B. Porten, *Archives from Elephantine: The Life of an Ancient Jewish Military Colony* (Berkeley: University of California Press, 1968). For a list of textual editions and bibliography, see Lester L. Grabbe, *Judaism from Cyrus to Hadrian* (Minneapolis: Fortress Press, 1992; London: SCM Press, 1994), pp. 53-55. Otherwise, our knowledge of the Jews is mainly from the Greek or Roman periods. Most of the original information on the Jews in Egypt in the Greek period is collected in V.A. Tcherikover, A. Fuks and M. Stern (eds.), *Corpus Papyrorum Judaicarum* (3 vols.; Cambridge, MA: Harvard University Press; Jerusalem: Magnes Press, 1957–64).

period, though the early Greek period cannot be excluded.[38] The main problem is that it deals with individuals alleged to be in the high echelons of government. Esther is queen and Mordechai is a high official. The Jewish community itself is not dealt with except as an entity under threat and then as an instrument of punishment on its enemies. Daniel 7–12 is dated by overwhelming evidence to the period of the Maccabaean revolt, but Daniel 1–6 may be a century or more earlier. The fact that the fourth kingdom in Dan. 2.40-43 clearly refers to the Greeks makes it unlikely that Daniel 1–6 is as early as the Persian period in its present form, though elements could perhaps be that early. Neither Esther nor Daniel seem to have reliable knowledge about the Persian period in general,[39] but the most serious defect is that neither gives any information about the Jews as a whole in Babylonia.

The book of Tobit is potentially the most helpful about conditions in which the exiles lived. It has some of the same problems as Esther and Daniel in that its knowledge of Mesopotamia is derivative and not first-hand.[40] But this is not all that important because, unlike Daniel and Esther (and also the story of Joseph), the events on the plane of government, the court and politics are not particularly significant in the book. These are mentioned in passing rather than being essential elements in the story. Although the story is set in the time of Assyrian rule, the book itself is no earlier than the Persian period because it not only knows of the fall of Nineveh and Jerusalem to the Babylonians (Tob. 14.4), but it is also aware of the rebuilding of the temple under the Persians (Tob. 14.5). On the other hand, it shows no knowledge of the coming of the Greeks. It is possible that this book was written before the conquests of Alexander. The main argument against a

---

38. S.B. Berg, *The Book of Esther: Motifs, Themes and Structure* (SBLDS, 44; Atlanta: Scholars Press, 1979), pp. 169-73, notes Hellenistic influences.

39. On Esther, a summary can be found in Carey A. Moore, *Esther* (AB, 7B; Garden City, NY: Doubleday, 1971). For Daniel, see John J. Collins, *Daniel* (Hermeneia; Minneapolis: Fortress Press, 1994). A good example of Daniel's lack of knowledge is 'Darius the Mede', on which see my 'Another Look at the *Gestalt* of "Darius the Mede"', *CBQ* 50 (1988), pp. 198-213. In general, see my article, 'Fundamentalism and Scholarship'.

40. The standard commentary on Tobit in English is now Carey A. Moore, *Tobit: A New Translation with Introduction and Commentary* (AB, 40a; New York: Doubleday, 1996). Cf. also my brief commentary on Tobit in J.W. Rogerson and J. Dunn (eds.), *Commentary 2000* (Grand Rapids: Eerdmans, forthcoming).

composition so early is the language of the Aramaic fragments from Qumran.[41]

The book of Tobit makes no grand claims for its main protagonists. They seem to be fairly ordinary people, though better off financially than the majority were likely to be. There is a great deal of emphasis on marriage within the tribe; in some contexts one could interpret this literally but others suggest a more general meaning of marriage with fellow 'Israelites'.[42] The focus of religion is the home. The festivals such as Shavuot (Pentecost) are kept within the family. Prayer is done privately. Piety is expressed in such activities as almsgiving, burying the dead and honouring one's parents.

Tobit fits in well with the conditions of the exiled communities under the Assyrians, Babylonians and Persians.[43] We know how many of the exiled peoples lived, and the Israelites and Jews must have been in a similar situation. One other source seems to mention some Jews specifically. This is the Murašû archive.[44] The Murašû house was a business and financial establishment, employing a number of servants

41. The Aramaic manuscripts from Qumran are basically the same sort of Aramaic known in other Qumran documents and thus later than the Achaemenid period (cf. Joseph A. Fitzmyer, 'The Aramaic and Hebrew Fragments of Tobit from Cave 4', *CBQ* 57 [1995], pp. 655-75, esp. p. 657). It is, of course, possible that the language of the book was updated at some point. A popular story might be more liable to such retelling in contemporary language than another genre of text. Also, we cannot be absolutely certain that the original language was Aramaic, though it is the most likely case from the data presently known (cf. Fitzmyer, 'The Aramaic and Hebrew Fragments', and J.D. Thomas, 'The Greek Text of Tobit', *JBL* 91 [1972], pp. 463-71).

42. The people are almost always referred to as Israelites in the book (1.18; 5.5, 9; 13.3), but Tob. 11.17 speaks of all 'the Jews' in Nineveh. This seems to be a slip of the pen which gives away the actual context, i.e. the Jewish diaspora rather than Israelites in Assyrian exile.

43. The situation under the Assyrians is described by Oded, *Mass Deportations*, especially pp. 75-115, but the situation of exiles under the Babylonians and Persians does not seem to have been particularly different. See also Oded, 'Observations on the Israelite/Judaean Exiles in Mesopotamia', pp. 205-12.

44. G. Cardascia, *Les archives des Murašû* (Paris: Imprimerie Nationale, 1951); Matthew W. Stolper, *Entrepeneurs and Empire: The Murašû Archive, the Murašû Firm, and Persian Rule in Babylonia* (Uitgaven van het Nederlands Historisch–Archaeologisch Instituut te Istanbul, 54; Leiden: Nederlands Historisch–Archaeologisch Instituut te Istanbul, 1985).

and agents. Some of these individuals seem to be Jewish, though this is based on the form of the names rather than direct identification.[45]

The Return of Exiles to Judah and Jerusalem[46]
Ezra describes a community in Judah which originates when the Persians allow the return of exiles from the Babylonian captivity. We have no external sources that describe or even refer to this event. However, it has been proposed that the biblical account is in part based on contemporary sources. If so, the lack of external confirmation may be irrelevant. The source of the information in Ezra is thus vital to an assessment of historicity.

Ezra 1–6 is really the key since it tells of the return of exiles to settle in and rebuild Judah and Jerusalem, but it is also very problematic.[47] The sources have been variously assessed. The argument that the author of Ezra 1–6 depended almost entirely on a few sources has been convincingly argued: the 'Cyrus decree' (1.2-4), a list of temple vessels (1.9–11), a genealogical and settlement list of uncertain origin (2.1-70), the books of Haggai and Zechariah, and a handful of Persian documents.[48] If correct, this means that the narrative of Ezra 3–6 is a creation of the author from these sources and thus has no independent value. The supposed decree of Cyrus (1.2-4) mentions return from exile, but despite some eminent defenders it is difficult to accept that this is anything more than the creation of a Jewish scribe.[49]

If this analysis is correct, we are left with only two sources in Ezra 1–6 which may resolve the question of whether an actual return of Jewish exiles took place. Ezra 2 has the character of a list of settlement rather than one of returnees and could represent a community made up of returnees over a considerable period of time. Nevertheless, it seems to presuppose a resettled community rather than just one which continued after the fall of Jerusalem. The other source is the Persian

45. M.D. Coogan, *West Semitic Personal Names in the Murašû Documents* (HSM, 7; Atlanta: Scholars Press, 1976).

46. My interpretation of this period and its sources as a whole is found in Ch. 2 of Grabbe, *Judaism from Cyrus to Hadrian*.

47. See my 'Reconstructing History from the Book of Ezra', in P.R. Davies (ed.), *Second Temple Studies*. I. *The Persian Period* (JSOTSup, 117; Sheffield: JSOT Press, 1991), pp. 98-107.

48. H.G.M. Williamson, 'The Composition of Ezra i-vi', *JTS* NS 34 (1983), pp. 1-30; *idem, Ezra, Nehemiah* (WBC, 16; Waco, TX: Word Books, 1985), p. xxiv.

49. Cf. Grabbe, *Judaism from Cyrus to Hadrian*, pp. 34-35.

documents which have often been taken as contemporary documents without further ado, but my study indicates that this cannot be done.[50] Although in some or even all cases, genuine Persian documents may have been used, in some or even all cases they have also been worked over by Jewish scribes. The one document that struck me as most likely to be authentic is that of Tattenai (Ezra 5.7-17). It attests that a Jewish community was rebuilding a temple in Jerusalem in the reign of Darius (most likely Darius I) and claimed to have been allowed to return by Cyrus. If this document is accepted as authentic, it is contemporary evidence for a Jerusalem community of returnees from the exile.

One passage of particular interest is Ezra 4, which tells about the 'adversaries' who oppose the building of the Jerusalem temple. In 4.2 they claim to have been brought to the land by Esarhaddon of Assyria. Possibly they but probably a different group write to the Persian king Artaxerxes and claim to be inhabitants of Erech, Babylon and Elam, who had been brought into Samaria and the surrounding region by 'Osnappar' (4.9-10). If authentic, as widely assumed, these passages provide very useful information about exile and deportation to the Palestinian area. Their historicity is not straightforward, however, because they both occur in a polemical context. That is, the author of this chapter is determined to label the 'adversaries' as foreigners;[51] therefore, he could simply be inventing a group that claims to have been brought in, a group that condemns itself as 'foreign' out of its own mouth, as it were. There is also the fact that they claim to have been brought in by Esarhaddon in 4.2, whereas no such deportation is known. Similarly, there is no such king as the Osnappar of 4.9-10, though this has been explained as a corruption of Ashurbanipal; however, there is no known deportation under Ashurbanipal. On the other hand, the fact that this information could not have been copied from a biblical text might argue for it as an authentic statement.

---

50. In a paper, 'The Authenticity of the Persian "Documents" in Ezra', read to the Aramaic Section of the Society of Biblical Literature annual meeting, San Francisco (November 1992).

51. As has often been suspected, it is likely that these 'adversaries' were simply the descendants of those who had not been deported in the first place and thus hardly foreigners. Cf. Robert P. Carroll, 'The Myth of the Empty Land', in David Jobling and Tina Pippin (eds.), *Ideological Criticism of Biblical Texts* (Semeia, 59; Atlanta: Scholars Press, 1992), pp. 79-93; Hans M. Barstad, *The Myth of the Empty Land: A Study in the History and Archaeology of Judah During the 'Exilic' Period* (Symbolae osloenses, 28; Oslo: Scandinavian University Press, 1996).

The question is, with such a problematic text can we have any confidence that there was a return of exiles? The fact of an exile from the Northern Kingdom and the Southern Kingdom is in part confirmed by Mesopotamian sources, and these same sources give considerable credence to the general biblical picture of the fall of both Samaria and Jerusalem. However, we do not have this same level confirmation for the return from exile. Is the return only a literary or even theological invention? There are several arguments that support the idea that some sort of return from exile took place:

1. Return of communities from exile to their homeland is known in a few instances (see first section of the article), so a return of Jewish exiles would not be unprecedented.

2. The list of Ezra 2/Nehemiah 7 suggests (at least, in part) a settlement pattern of returnees rather than that of people who continued to remain in the land after the Babylonian conquest.

3. The letter of Tattenai in Ezra 5.7-17 has a number of marks of authenticity. Its Aramaic has the features of Achaemenid Aramaic known from Persian documents and none of the later features.[52] The information in it about Sheshbazzar goes contrary to the narrative in Ezra 3–6 (which makes the return and rebuilding the work of Zerubbabel and Joshua) and even the account of Sheshbazzar in Ezra 1 (where he has only the job of bringing the temple vessels back). In 5.16 Sheshbazzar not only is governor of the province but he also starts the work of rebuilding the temple, long before Zerubbabel is on the scene.

4. The problem is not really that some exiles returned even though the majority seem to have remained in Babylonia. The problem is that those who were never exiled are ignored at best or treated as 'foreigners' and 'enemies' at worst, as has been well laid out.[53] It would seem unnecessary to create a 'myth of the empty land' if no one had ever returned from exile.

52. Discussed in Grabbe, 'The Authenticity of the Persian "Documents" in Ezra' (n. 50 above).
53. See n. 51 above.

5.   Ezra and Nehemiah are not the only evidence for a return.
      Isaiah 40–55 is almost universally dated to the exilic period. If
      this is correct, it is a genuine prophecy, predicting that Cyrus
      would give the Jews permission to return to their land. The
      idealistic picture of this return in 40.1-5, 43.16-2, and 51.9-11
      is touching but hardly realistic. Therefore, we can take these
      as expectations, not descriptions of what actually happened;
      yet it shows that there were Jews who wanted—and
      expected—to return. However, it has recently been argued that
      Deutero–Isaiah should be dated to the reign of Xerxes.[54] If
      this is correct, Isaiah 40–55 is a contemporary source and is
      not just predicting a return but is actually expressing (albeit in
      a *vaticinia ex eventu* and in idealistic terms) a known return of
      Jewish exiles back to the home country. If we understand
      Deutero–Isaiah from *either* perspective, it would be difficult to
      reject the idea of some sort of return from exile. Despite the
      problems with Ezra 1–6, Deutero–Isaiah provides consider-
      able support for some sort of return.

6.   The return of Jews from exile is rather more specific than one
      might expect for a purely theological creation. Only members
      of the Southern Kingdom return, not those from the Northern
      Kingdom. It is also clear that only a small portion of those in
      captivity return. The 'myth' created by the biblical writer is
      that of the empty land, not of a return of a small portion of the
      exiles.

Conclusions about Historical Methodology

From the discussion above I would draw the following conclusions
about matters of historical method:

(1) The biblical text must not be ignored. Its authors/editors sometimes had considerable accurate information. This is evidently the case
with 2 Kings in regard to the events surrounding the fall of Samaria and
the fall of Jerusalem. What the source of that information was (whether

54. Philip R. Davies, 'God of Cyrus, God of Israel: Some Religio-Historical
Reflections on Isaiah 40–55', in Jon Davies, Graham Harvey and Wilfred G.E.
Watson (eds.), *Words Remembered, Texts Renewed: Essays in Honour of John F.A.
Sawyer* (JSOTSup, 195; Sheffield: Sheffield Academic Press, 1995), pp. 207-25.

national archives, temple archives or whatever) is not known, but we have to accept the fact of this knowledge. In other cases, the knowledge is questionable or even to be considered inaccurate or non-existent. Thus, no blanket judgment can be made about the biblical text. It may be an important historical source, it may be in the nature of a historical novel (or novelistic history, if one prefers), or it may be a literary construct out of whole cloth. Of course, these three positions are only points on a spectrum in which every shade of possibility from accuracy to invention is represented.

(2) The biblical text should not be rejected just because it is part of a theological/religious document—nor should it be accepted for the same reasons. It has to be evaluated, carefully and critically, in each individual situation. A case needs to be made for whatever position one takes, and the case needs to be made for each individual text. Generalized judgments, whether pro or con, will not do.

(3) It is perfectly legitimate to draw conclusions and to make reconstructions from the data available, even if these are very few. The fact that we cannot be certain is no reason to dismiss a reconstruction or hypothesis.[55] Even very tentative data and surmises can be used if one is honest about what one is doing. Plausibility has a place, as well. The fact that something is plausible is not the same as saying it is demonstrated, but plausibility is a first stage in the process of argument.

(4) The nature of any reconstruction or hypothesis needs to be made plain. The more assured the data, the more assured the hypothesis, and vice versa. In the matter of the exile, our knowledge of the details (such as we have them) of what happened preceding and during the fall of Samaria and Jerusalem is on more solid ground than what happened about the return of exiles during the early Persian period. I think we can have a good deal of confidence in reconstructing what happened in Judah in the two decades preceding the fall of Jerusalem, even where 2 Kings (and, to some extent, Jeremiah) are our only sources. I feel much less confident about the situation described in Ezra 1–6, though I think the broad outline there can be worked out with some degree of

55. Cf. the remarks of Donald B. Redford, 'A Response to Anson Rainey's "Remarks on Donald Redford's *Egypt, Canaan, and Israel in Ancient Times*"', *BASOR* 301 (Feb. 1996), pp. 77-81, in particular p. 77: '...it behooves the historian of the Levant in the second millennium BC not to be ashamed to admit ignorance, but label all reconstructions as educated guesses to be relinquished at a moment's notice'.

probability. I would reject any position which refuses to use the biblical text in historical reconstruction relating to the exile or which maintains a purely agnostic stance, just as I would also reject any position that accepts the biblical text unless it can be disproved.

So, can I write a history of 'the exile'? Yes, I believe I can, and I do not believe it would be 'bogus history'.[56] Without going into all the details I would want to consider, such a history would go something like this:

First, there were two exiles of people from 'Israel', from Samaria and the Northern Kingdom in 722 BCE and from Jerusalem and Judah in 597 and 587–586 BCE. We also know there were exiles of other peoples (e.g. the Philistine cities) from Syria/Palestine during the period of Assyrian and Babylonian rule, though I have not attempted to catalogue them here.[57] How many people were exiled is not clear, though it seems evident that a considerable portion of the population remained in the land. For example, Sargon II mentions only 27,000 from Samaria, which could not have been the whole population.[58] We know that exiled communities need not lose their identity, and occasional returns of exiles are attested.

The exile of the Northern Kingdom has already been dealt with in detail by a member of the Seminar and need not detain us.[59] The events leading up to the exile are known in comparative detail. This conquest and exile is typical of deportations carried out under Assyrian rule. Once the exile had taken place, we lose sight of those taken away. The mention of 'Samarians' in Mesopotamia is found in a number of Assyrian documents, but the numbers actually mentioned are few and

56. This is the term used for certain sorts of invented history by Robert P. Carroll, 'Madonna of Silences: Clio and the Bible', in Lester L. Grabbe (ed.), *Can a History of Israel Be Written?* (European Seminar in Historical Methodology, 1; JSOTSup, 245; Sheffield: Sheffield Academic Press, 1997), pp. 84-103.

57. Many of these are referred to in Oded, *Mass Deportations*.

58. The matter is naturally quite complicated. There is the question of the accuracy of numbers of deportees in Assyrian inscriptions; one would like to know whether the figure is meant to apply to all the country or only the city of Samaria; and there is the debate about whether further deportations took place over a period of time. Cf. N. Na'aman, 'Population Changes in Palestine Following Assyrian Deportations', *Tel Aviv* 29 (1993), pp. 104-24.

59. Becking, *The Fall of Samaria*; his study is in the way of prolegomena, however, since he does not actually write a history of the period as such.

do not necessarily arise from deportation in every case.[60] The conditions of those in exile can only be surmised, but we have a general picture of the situation in which exiles found themselves.[61] Similarly, we do not know precisely the peoples brought into Samaria, though the list in 2 Kgs 17.24 is plausible, and Sargon's inscriptions mention some Arab tribes (which may be a bit later).

The events leading up to the fall of Jerusalem are also known in a good deal of detail compared to many other periods of history. The Babylonian sources cover the period between 610 and 594 BCE quite well. The picture in 2 Kings and, to a lesser extent, Jeremiah fit into this outline very neatly. Therefore, after 594 when there is little confirmation, the account in 2 Kings (and parts of Jeremiah) is quite credible. Whether the details can be believed is subject to further investigation, but the essential picture could be as accurate as it is only if the writer had some reliable source of information, whatever that might have been. Even some incidental details are supported indirectly by contemporary sources.[62]

Some indication of the conditions and situation of the Jewish exile may be gleaned from a few brief passing references in Babylonian sources (e.g. the Murašû documents and the Jehoiachin tablet), the analogy from the data in Assyrian sources, and possibly from the book of Tobit. Perhaps the most difficult area for trying to write a history is the alleged return of Jewish exiles to Judah and Jerusalem. Yet I believe we can assert with considerable confidence that such a return took place, though the details of how, when, and their relationship to the non-exiled population are moot points.[63] On the other hand, most of the exiled community remained in Mesopotamia, though they seem to have kept their identity and contacts with their fellows in Judah.[64]

The biblical concept of exile and return was, therefore, based on actual events. Although exile and return form a significant theological

60. Eph'al, '"The Samarian(s)" in the Assyrian Sources'.

61. Oded, *Mass Deportations*, pp. 75-115.

62. See n. 33 above.

63. My own discussion and interpretation can be found in Ch. 2 of *Judaism from Cyrus to Hadrian*, in *Ezra–Nehemiah* (London: Routledge, 1998), and in my projected study, *Yehud: The Persian Province of Judah*.

64. Unfortunately, much of the information before the Roman period is found only in late rabbinic texts. Much of this information is dealt with by Jacob Neusner, *A History of the Jews in Babylonia*. I. *The Parthian Period* (Leiden: E.J. Brill, 1969; repr. BJS, 62; Atlanta: Scholars Press, 1984).

theme in the biblical text, they were not just made up for theological purposes. In this particular case, the theology represents an interpretation and reuse of historical events.

THE EXILE IN HISTORY AND MYTH:
A RESPONSE TO HANS BARSTAD[1]

Thomas L. Thompson

Hans Barstad's recent monograph, *The Myth of the Empty Land*,[2] poses an interesting question for future study. For the moment, this study offers a middle ground in the current debates on historiography and biblical historicity. Unfortunately, Barstad confuses the categories of modern historiography and ancient literature. This allows him to speculate on the historicity of the 'empty land'. For Barstad, history remains one of the exilic period of Isaiah on his principle of 'lack of disbelief'. In contrast to the scepticism expressed in this regard, Barstad's own disbelief regarding Nehemiah's empty land seems odd. I have never assumed a relationship between belief and history and I hope the following review offers a means of separating the two. It is unfortunate that Barstad's use of archaeology for historical purposes does not carry us beyond the historicity debate, which is more appropriate to a theological world of biblical archaeology than to an investigation related to the history of Palestine. While it may be true that archaeology does not confirm that the whole of Jerusalem went into exile in 586, we might point out that the questions he asks of archaeology are more than it can answer. These are literary questions.

It is not that I can argue against Barstad and claim that all or most of Jerusalem was carried off to Babylon in 586. I know nothing of that; not even that it was destroyed at this time. In the following, what I do try to do is expand on our ignorance of this historical period and make

---

1.   This paper is abstracted from Chapter 9 of my forthcoming book, *The Bible and History*, to be published by Cape (London) in 1999.

2.   Hans M. Barstad, *The Myth of the Empty Land: A Study in the History and Archaeology of Judah during the 'Exilic' Period* (Symbolae osloenses, 28 Oslo: Scandinavian University Press, 1996).

an effort to separate the two quite different worlds of history and the Bible. In this, I hope that the issues gain in focus.

Historical Sources

Apart from the traditions of Israel's origins, there are two great defining story periods that have influenced the Bible's perception of an old Israel which formed its description of the past. The period of the 'united monarchy' was a great golden age, comparable in many ways to King Arthur's old England. It was centered on the figure of David, the heroic and eponymous ancestor and founder of Jerusalem's 'House of David' (which, much like the house of Omri in Samaria, was the historical name of Jerusalem's patronate). This 'House of the Beloved', not only evoked the temple as the center of his old Israel's story, but found in the stories about David a fictional representation of Yahweh's eternal rule over his people from Zion, his holy mountain. This was Israel lost. The other tradition centers on the 'exile and return', which is a defining 'origin story' of a 'new Israel'. This origin story is equally legendary. Following the mythical motifs of the phoenix, the exile carries us through the death of the old Israel to the resurrection of the new, and it is through these motifs of dying and rebirth that the stories take on their substance in the Bible's vision of the past. Critical histories of this period have largely failed; for evidence for the history of this period—beginning with the fall of Jerusalem in 586—is much like historical evidence for the tenth century. Most of its historical trees have fallen unheeded, and we know little of them.

The common imperial policy in the ancient Near East of population transference was first of all a policy of 'pacification'. It was a military strategy that has been used by armies throughout history. Armies change and transform the societies of the regions they enter. Such changes are rarely, if ever, undone. While generals crush opposition and resistance to their occupying armies as a matter of course, there are considerable variations in the efficiency with which this is done. The variance is often not best explained by the simple brutality or compassion of those issuing orders; other factors often play a more important role. Some of the factors that played a role in the policies of Assyria's generals were the safety, morale and discipline of their troops; creating fear and terror within the conquered territories wherever the army's hold on a region suffered resistance; destroying the integrity of the indigenous society and leadership that showed itself resistant or potentially resistent to Assyrian policy; reducing hatred of the occupying forces by presenting the army as agents of positive change; creating dependency and loyalty to the imperial administration; fulfilling short- and long-range plans to integrate the territory into the imperial adminis- tration; rebuilding the social fabric of the territories wherever des- troyed; supplying the needs of other regions of the empire; filling the expansive demands of the army itself for new troops; creating eco- nomic monopolies of skilled tradesmen in Assyria's cities; and main- taining support for war at home by satisfying the needs of the cities for cheap labor and profits.

Important to a successful outcome of these truly complex policies was the behavior and the attitude of the people who came under the control of the army. The massive population transference involved in such policies of deportation was an ancient war crime, condemned and criticized long before the poems of the book of Amos were written. This 'pacification of the countryside' had been a practice of armies since at least Egypt's Old Kingdom in the Early Bronze Age. Cyrus was hardly the first imperialist to learn that his purposes could be achieved even more effectively if he could change the understanding of those he conquered. Loyalties could be created through advertisement, through propaganda. Arguments were developed to persuade people to accept what was being done to them. Whenever possible they should welcome it. Combining propaganda with terror proved doubly effec- tive. The execution of 'past oppressors' and 'enemies of the people' was infinitely more effective than doing away with the leaders of the people and the enemies of Assyria. Policies were created to alienate people from their rulers. Combined with selective executions as impli- cit warnings of the consequences of disobedience, such reinterpretation of reality was profoundly effective in the creation of loyalties. The fre- quent use of enslavement, the threat of starvation and the separation of families effectively silenced the voices of independent thought.

Ancient siege warfare leant itself readily to this kind of psychological war. 'Carrots' could be and were also used: from the promise of food and water, plans for reuniting families that had been separated, promises of land to the hopes of a new life—all created believers in a new past. The habitual self-presentation of the conquering army as an army of liberation whose generals became near-cosmic saviors—hardly modern—is also a constant feature of this propaganda. In the sixteenth century the Pharaoh Ahmose had described himself in this role as he drove the 'hated' Hyksos from the land, whom he described as foreigners who had shamelessly oppressed the people. Centuries later, an Assyrian general, conquering a village in the Lebanon (an area in which the Assyrian army had never been before), presented himself as the liberator of the village. He destroyed the 'brutal thief' (namely, the village chief), who had oppressed them for so long. This same general deported the entire population of another town while telling the people that he was returning them to their 'original home' and to their 'original lands', from which they had been uprooted by their oppressors long before. The Babylonians rebuilt the formerly great Assyrian trading center of Harran in northern Mesopotamia. In a dedicatory inscription, the Babylonian king explains to the people that Śin, the ancient god of Harran, had ordered him to restore the god to his house in Harran, and to return the people to their homes and to their true worship, which the (former) Assyrian administration had allowed to go to ruin. The people who are given to understand themselves as 'returned' were, in fact, deportees from Arabia, from Elam (i.e. Afghanistan) and from Egypt. When in their turn the Babylonians were defeated, they were subject to the same propaganda at the hands of the Persians. They were accused of having abandoned 'right religion' and of having allowed the gods and the temples to go to ruin. In fact, the anger among the gods which this neglect of religion had created, is given as the reason for the Babylonians' defeat. The new Persian emperor, Cyrus, puts himself forward as the protector of traditional religion throughout the empire. He is the liberator of those who had been enslaved by the Babylonians. Even Babylon itself is described as having opened its gates to his army and having welcomed his arrival. Not only did the Bible's Yahweh, but also other gods appeared to Cyrus to give him instructions concerning their peoples. They ordered him—who as conquering king of kings presents himself in the humble role of servant of the gods—to restore people to their homelands, to rebuild the homes (temples) of the gods, and to re-establish the societies that the Babylonians had left in ruins. This is the language of propaganda, the language of deportation and population transference. People were uprooted and, with all the goods they had in the world on their backs, were forced to move thousands of miles to a land in which they had never been. In such a condition those who had 'returned' from exile to their ancient 'home' in Jerusalem came to understand themselves.

The Bible and related traditions associate Israel and Judah with imperial policies of massive population transference more than a dozen different times. Some of these transports have also been confirmed by extra-biblical records. The first three were at the hands of the Assyrians. In his campaign of 733–732, Tiglath-pileser deports people from several towns in northern Palestine in connection with his conquest of Damascus. These towns, including Hazor, are understood in the biblical narratives to belong to Israel, but also involve regions in the Galilee and Gilead. In 722, the Assyrians under Shalmanezer took Samaria. In transforming the region to a province, they transferred people from the region to Assyria: to 'Halah on the Habur, the valley of Gozan and to the cities of the Medes'. They also transferred peoples into the region; including people from Hamath and Babylon (2 Kings 17). The third population transfer under the Assyrians occurs during the reign of Sennacherib. This mentions only the deportation of peoples from the region. It is said to have affected Jerusalem, Judah and the coastal plain in the campaign that destroyed the town of Lachish in 701. There are at least two (Jeremiah refers to three) other transferences of people away from the area under the Babylonians in 597 and then what is often described as a final destruction of Jerusalem and deportation under Nebuchadnezzar in 586. However, we must notice that 2 Kings' description of Jerusalem's fall includes two successive deportations in which *all the people* were carried off. This, however, still allowed enough for 'all the people small and great' to escape to Egypt after the assassination of the Assyrian appointed Gedalaiah (2 Kings 25).[3] Four further transferences occur in the stories of Ezra and Nehemiah and are attributed to the Persian period. These are said to occur under Cyrus (538), Darius I (521–485), Artaxerxes I (464–423) and Artaxerxes II (404–358). These refer only to transferences of population to the territory from Babylon. Traditions also refer to population transferences in the early Hellenistic period, from the city of Samaria by Alexander to Egypt and to the city of Samaria (Sebaste) from Macedonia. The opening column of the *Damascus Document*, found in Cairo and at Qumran, refers to an Ezra-like figure, the 'teacher of righteousness' who brought 'a remnant of Israel' back some 390 years after they had been deported by Nebuchadnezzar. The Jewish rebellions of 67–70 and 135 CE against the Romans each, in their turn, involved comparable policies of population

---

3. Much in the same way, the plague stories of Exodus are able to kill off all of the Egyptian cattle twice.

transference. Finally, Samaritan traditions, known from medieval texts, include a tradition of return from exile to Samaria as well as a return tradition of the Jews to Jerusalem.

Without arguing that each of these traditions is accurate—it is clear that they are not—there is enough evidence and confirmation from independent records to understand the biblical stories as reflective of imperial policies from the Assyrian through the Roman period. The traditions reflect what was a staple of imperial military policy for over a thousand years. No single tradition alone is enough to say that any specific event certainly occurred. Yet, such events and their implications for social coherence and identity were part of the fabric of the society of Palestine under imperial control.

We have no proven connection between any of the known deportations and a corresponding 'return', and we have much reason to assume that such connections are rather the results of interpretation and understanding. Similarly, we have sufficient reason to assume that deportations from Samaria or Jerusalem were hardly total. The literary motif of total deportation is hyperbolic, expressive of the totality of the disaster. This is just as true for the account of the fall of Samaria in 722 and of Jerusalem in 586 BCE as it is for Jerusalem of 70 and 135 CE. We also have much reason to believe that such transferences were multilateral. In the case of Samaria in 722, we have Assyrian records offering evidence of populations transferred to Israel. The stability of regional economies alone would demand a minimum of reciprocity. Archaeological surveys for sixth-century Judah and estimates regarding Jerusalem's population in the fifth, suggest that such was the case in Jerusalem after the deportations of the early sixth century. A substantial continuity of the society can often be suggested by the history of settlement and lack of major disruption or change in the material culture. The indigenous material culture continues to dominate after such disruptions. At the same time, disruption and radical transformation should also be confirmed.

On the level of individuals and of local town societies, the trend of change over centuries from locally indigenous regional cultures to an imperial society is overwhelming. Those who had been imported into Palestine to replace deportees were part of a recurrent process of integration with the host region. As they integrated, they came to identify themselves with that group. At times, as in Samaria, this identification was through an understanding of themselves as people who had always lived in the region. At times, as in groups moved in large numbers to such a non-West Semitic area as Babylon, or as in groups who maintained an identity opposed to the local population as in military colonies of West Semitic soldiers established in Egypt, identity took the form of understanding oneself as living in a diaspora: away from one's homeland. At times, as in Jerusalem, it came through the bulk of the population coming to understand themselves as exiles who had returned to their original homeland. At yet other times, completely new identities were created. At all times, however, such understanding began with the need of understanding and interpreting one's situation through a description of the past. Both politically and literarily, this was done quite independently from whatever that past might actually have been.

In every deportation and resettlement, the rebuilding of the infrastructures of a society was faced with the problems of integrating the refugees or deportees into an established society that had very little reason to welcome them. In the case of Samaria and Jerusalem, at least five major long-term effects resulted from such difficulties: (1) The language of Aramaic, the official international language of the Assyrian, Babylonian and Persian empires, became a viable language in Palestine. It was, perhaps, the only language with which the linguistically very diverse groups in Palestine could communicate with each other and with imperial officials. (2) The process of unifying the people of Palestine, and especially the province of Jehud, through the development of common traditions of origins, was largely successful. By the end of the early second or the third century, this had already encouraged people in the province—whatever their historical origins—to accept as their own the ancestral tradition of having returned as Jews from Babylon. There were also many quite diverse people in Palestine and from Palestine who came to identify themselves around the quite distinct religious and traditional concept of being descendants of ancient Israel. Many frequently understood this in a sectarian way and found identification of themselves as a 'new' or as a 'true' Israel, rejecting others as 'old' and as 'false'. (3) Some of the conflicts between some groups of returnees and more 'indigenous' groups were never resolved. Ironically, the Jerusalem tradition reflected in the stories of Nehemiah, Ezra and Josephus understood some of these conflicts as due to the foreign roots which this tradition attributed to the whole of Samaria's population. (4) The separate and distinctive tradition of Samaria resisted integration into a trans-Palestinian identification of 'Judaism'. While Jerusalem shared Samaria's Pentateuch and many other story traditions, each group maintained its own cultic center. Once the different biblical traditions were developed during the Maccabean and early Roman periods, most other regionally identifiable groups both within Palestine and in the diaspora adopted one or other form of this Bible as their own origin tradition. (5) Finally, ideological differences between the self-identities of different, at times regionally defined groups, led to competitive and irreconcilable assertions of many groups of both Palestine and the diaspora to be the sole 'legitimate' heirs of Israel. These conflicts confirmed the sectarian nature of most groups who were claiming this tradition as their own.

Contrary to expectations, a reading of the Bible as history does not become easier as we come closer to the historical contexts of the texts that form the traditions, only more frustrating. Books such as Ezra and Nehemiah in the Bible, 1 and 2 Maccabees and 1 Esdras in the apocrypha, Qumran's Damascus covenant and Josephus's *Antiquities of the Jews* possessed a great freedom in writing about the past. They told stories about the past whenever they had a story about the past to tell. These stories are recycled as if they were true accounts of the past. Many were made up in the hope of weaving a continuous narrative. They answer questions that were related to their own world, and their authors were rewarded for their cleverness and for the grace and power of their writing. Precious little is known about the past except for these stories, and most modern historical scholarship paraphrases one or other author of choice, usually for no other reason than that they are thought believable. That is, because they are good stories.

These works are not very different from the collections of texts and traditions about the apparently far more distant past. These we find in the Pentateuch, Jubilees, the books of Joshua–2 Kings and in 1–2 Chronicles and Daniel. The theme of origins, with its central functions of tradition collection and philosophical discussion, is oriented more towards techniques of balance and reiteration than to criticism and historical warrant. What is theologically and philosophically true takes precedence over whatever might have been known about the past. In 2 Kings, we find stories about the past. These formed the heart of its interest in the past. In a classic form of a folktale's ever-ironic claim to being historical, 2 Kings again and again delights in offering footnote references to imaginary royal archives (such as the 'Chronicles of the

Kings of Israel') for any who might be interested in what 2 Kings is not.

When later writers, such as the author of 2 Maccabees, and Josephus, follow in this vein with references to 'sources'—especially to sources we no longer have and many of which may never have existed—we must remember that, whatever the truth to such claims, we have access to the worlds of 2 Maccabees and Josephus only from the perspectives which they allow us. When 2 Maccabees 2, for example, opens for us the 'records' and the 'writing' about Jeremiah to talk about teaching the law of Moses to the people or of hiding the ark of the covenant on Moses' mountain until a time that 'god shows his mercy and gathers his people again', we can draw one of two conclusions. The author is either creating or he is transmitting pious fictions in support of the tradition's claim that the Mosaic tradition lives on after the exile. In neither case do we learn anything of a historical Jeremiah—only of the Jeremiah of story and legend. Similarly, when Josephus tells us of a letter written centuries earlier by Aristeas that recounts the origin of the Greek translation of Jewish traditions in Alexandria by 70 elders, we must not imagine that we are learning anything about the origins of the Greek Bible. We learn only what is implicit in Josephus's accounts: of the existence of the Greek bible *in Josephus's time* and of an effort—whether Josephus's own or his source's—to mark this translation as authentic and divinely inspired. Josephus, himself, undermines trust in Aristeas's letter, when he recounts the same legend in the form of a speech of Aristeas.

The problem of the fragmentation and ignorance of nearly every aspect of the history of the Persian and Hellenistic periods, as of any of our so-called biblical periods, is serious. The lack of primary sources, together with a wealth of literary and theological discourse, render this Second Temple period nearly inaccessible to history. Our secondary sources, however, are many and varied and give us a wealth of story. It is not that we know nothing of the past. Rather, what we do not have is any coherent narrative, either from the Bible or any other contemporary writer, which can offer any structure to our history of this period. We are left with a fragmented and a doubtful past.

The Myth of Exile

With the metaphor of exile in the Bible, the central problem has never been a lack of evidence for believing whether a historical situation in fact once existed. Deportation texts alone and the extensive imperial policies of population transference that were carried out over a period of more than a thousand years is more than an adequate foundation with which the Bible's literary metaphor of exile might find resonance in its audience. Many of these texts evoke an emotional and intellectual interpretation of such reference, as political and personal perceptions of 'exile'. This same emotional resonance is already implicit in the historical propaganda of the Babylonian king Nabonidus or of the Persian Cyrus in their claims of returning people and their gods to their homes. Such passion is dramatically captured in 2 Kings' story of the Assyrian general at Jerusalem's walls, offering the people exile 'that they might live and not die'. No, the problem is not whether there was ever a historical exile; nor has it ever been that the Bible's stories are not believable. There was exile... often.

The historical problems arise with the question of continuity: the continuity of people, of their culture and their traditions. When we read the Bible's narratives, are we looking at the means by which a culture and a tradition created continuity and coherence because of and out of the discontinuities of the people's experiences? Are the emotions of exile evoked in the implied feelings of those who were uprooted and deported different or comparable to those implied perceptions of people of another generation, or even centuries later, who heard the messages of a saving Nabonidus and Cyrus? When Shalmanezer took Samaria, were the people he deported from Samaria to live in Halah in Northern Mesopotamia 'returning' home? Or did they, too, live in exile, perhaps to 'return' to Jerusalem under Artaxerxes? Or did the people Shalmanezer brought *to* Samaria from the Syrian town of Hamath think of themselves as being forced to live in exile? While yet others 'returned?' And how did the people of Samaria see themselves three hundred years later? And Judah's exiles under Sennacherib, did they return? Or did anyone return? Or were those who understood themselves as having returned and whose traditions are celebrated in story a half-millennium later, in fact, brought to Judah by Sennacherib or to Jerusalem by Nebuchadnezzar, rather than by the later Cyrus, Darius or Alexander? And how could the authors of 1 Esdras or 2 Isaiah know? What we have in the Bible's stories of deportation, exile and return are not accounts of a past at all but a perfect example of how literature plays with the metaphors that experience has created for us. It is to this literary play, to the myth of exile, that we should now turn in asking about the quality of this biblical tradition which is so firmly and unquestionably 'anchored in history'.

For all the importance of the remnant theology surrounding the stories of Judah's return from exile in Babylon as a metaphor of divine mercy, we must never forget that this metaphor's closest variant is that of Israel's and Judah's total destruction. This formed a chain of tradition that survived just as vigorously as that of 'return'. This variant with its associations with motifs of 'new life' finds its center in the metaphor of a 'new Israel'. The well-known 'root of Jesse' motif of Isaiah is a closely related metaphor that plays on the image of the dead stump of the Davidic dynasty that lies just as firmly within the heart of exile poetry as does the alternative theme of continuity and return. Central to the revival of this tree is the Old Testament hope in what is a theology of resurrection. It is only in a historical world that such contrasting metaphors as death and survival are marked as contradictory. In literature, the motifs of resurrection, rebirth and return are complementary variations of a tradition's coherent vigor. Hardly contradictory, they are functional equivalents. This we shall see.

A related problem for those interested in history of an exile is the seeming lack of fixed substance in some of the literary perceptions of the exile: both of the idea of an exilic period and of the metaphor as such. We have, in fact, no narrative about the exile in the Bible. We do have alternative stories, such as the doublet-stories of Israel's enslavement in Egypt which leads to the Exodus story of return, and of Israel's 40 years of being tested in the wilderness followed by (re-) entry into the land of a new generation. We also have stories of going into exile and stories about coming out. But the history of the exile is a history written on blank pages. That we do not have an exilic narrative must at least raise for us the question of whether any such historical event of the past is in fact the reference of the traditions we do have. Is it possible that this one indisputable period of the Bible's history is a period about which the Bible shows no interest in making part of its narrative?

The book of Nehemiah opens when the Persian courtier Nehemiah hears of Jerusalem's disaster: that 'the walls had fallen and that the gates had been burned'. This news of Jerusalem's emptiness leads to a prayer of repentance in which Nehemiah plays the dramatic role of representing in his prayer 'all who would return to god with repentance and keep his commandments'. The god of heaven hears his prayers. When he repeats his lament to King Artaxerxes and asks permission to rebuild the city, it is granted. The theme of Jerusalem's total destruction—turned into a desert by the wrath of God—is a very important one theologically, where it carries out a double function. On one hand, it marks Jerusalem's destruction as the final movement of the deity's exhausted patience in the chain of stories of ever-recurrent human rebellion that had begun in Genesis. This final destruction, complete and unforgiving, is the punishment long threatened and delayed, that had been promised as far back as Exodus 23. In the wilderness, Yahweh had promised Moses: 'I send my angel before you to guard you and to bring you to the place I have prepared.' This guardian spirit, however, is hardly a beneficent creature, but takes on something of the role of a mafia-like enforcer, evocative of *1 Enoch*'s 'watchers': 'Listen to him and respond to his voice; do not rebel against him; for he will not forgive your crime. My name is in him.' So, this long-distant prophecy of Jerusalem's destruction is recalled in the language of desolation and in the image of Jerusalem as wilderness. On the other hand, it is also this same wilderness metaphor that leads Nehemiah to repent on behalf of the people. This repentance leads to Jerusalem's renewal and rebirth, as Nehemiah takes on the role of Yahweh's angel who now leads this new 'Israel' to the place that God has prepared.

These same interlocking motifs of destruction, wilderness and return are found in the metaphor of Isaiah's great exodus song of return in Isaiah 40 that so famously captures the suffering of Jerusalem's exile in his great poem of consolation: 'Give comfort, give comfort to my people, says your god. Speak tenderly to Jerusalem. Cry out to her that her slavery is over. Her crime is forgiven; for she has received at Yahweh's hand, double for her sins... A voice cries in the wilderness: prepare Yahweh's path; make straight the way of God through the desert.' In his book, it is Nehemiah's voice that cries from Jerusalem's wilderness and goes to prepare the way.

Jeremiah's book of Lamentations also builds the same kind of theology from Jerusalem's loss. It visits not Babylon, but rather impoverished Jerusalem (1.1-3). Lamentations opens with the motif of the emptiness of Jerusalem: 'How lonely sits the city that was full of people! How like a widow she has become, she that was great among the nations...' That the text speaks of the exile as present is clear in v. 3: 'Judah has gone into exile in affliction and hard labor. Now she dwells as one among the nations, but she finds no rest...' In ch. 2, we read of Jerusalem's destruction and of the deportation of its leaders: 'Her gates have fallen to the ground; he has ruined and broken her bars; her kings and princes are among the nations; the law is no more and her prophets obtain no vision from Yahweh.' The poems speak of great suffering, of death and of despair: 'In the dust of the streets lie the young and the old; maids and young men have fallen by the sword; in the day of your [i.e. God's] anger, you have killed them, slaughtering without mercy... On the day of Yahweh's anger, none escaped; none survived.' Jeremiah speaks for all of Jerusalem. 'I am one who has seen suffering; he has brought me darkness without light... He has forced me to live in darkness like the dead of long ago.' The image is of Jerusalem as a desert: 'How like a desert this city that was full of people.' Yet, this empty Jerusalem is a theological Jerusalem, not a historical one.

Chapter 5 opens with a summation of Jerusalem's disgrace in the voice of its people: 'Our inheritance has been turned over to strangers, our homes to aliens. We have become orphans, fatherless; our mothers are like widows. We must pay for the water we drink; the wood we get must be bought. With a yoke on our neck we are hard driven...' The desert is not an empty but a moral wilderness. In fact, the city is filled with people...and crime:

> Women are raped in Zion; virgins in the villages of Judah; princes are hung up by their hands. No respect is shown elders; young men are forced to grind at the mill and boys stagger under loads of wood; the old have quit the city gate and the young their music. The joy of our hearts has ceased; our dancing has turned to mourning. Zion is a wilderness. Jackals prowl.

This exilic Jerusalem of the wilderness, this city in the hands of the godless, where women are raped and heroes hung, is the same Jerusalem that is visited by Jeremiah's scorn: 'Run back and forth through the streets of Jerusalem, look and take note! Search her squares to see if you can find a man; one who does justice and seeks truth; that I may pardon her.' The scene echoes Abraham's confrontation with Yahweh in Genesis 18: 'Suppose there are fifty righteous; will you then destroy the place and not spare it for the sake of the fifty righteous?' At the debate's closure, Yahweh declares that for the sake of ten—a blessed minyan, the number required for public prayer—he will not destroy it. Sodom, like Jerusalem, *is* destroyed.

Just as the story of Sodom and Gomorrah's destruction epitomizes Jerusalem of the exile, in Jeremiah's Lamentations, the wilderness as godless chaos subject to Yahweh's destruction, marks this same

Jerusalem of the exile as a wilderness of the soul seeking repentance. This becomes very clear when we read a poem in Hosea, ch. 2, that is about Israel rather than Jerusalem. The song has much in common with ch. 5 of Lamentations. In this poem, Israel is portrayed as Hosea's wife, a prostitute, whose children are named 'my people' and 'she is granted pity'. The poem opens with Hosea playing the role of Yahweh speaking to the children:

> Plead with your mother, plead—for she is not my wife, and I am not her husband—that she remove her whoring from her face; her adultery from her breasts: that I not strip her naked and make her as on the day of her birth; that I not make her a desert; turn her into a wilderness and kill her with thirst...

The poem presents a picture of Israel's destruction by Yahweh as a punishment for turning to the worship of Ba'al. In the closure of the poem, however, the theme of wilderness returns. The wilderness now reiterates the wilderness of the Exodus; it becomes a place of testing, of repentance and forgiveness: as a doorway of hope and return: a promise of Israel's rebirth:

> Look, I will seduce her and bring her out to the wilderness; there I will speak tenderly to her: I will return to her her vineyards and make the Achor Valley a doorway of hope. She will respond to me as she did when she was young; when she came up out of the land of Egypt.

Historiography and the past is abandoned in these verses as the song turns to the universals of the soul's relationship to its god. The theme of wilderness as the place of repentance and turning to Yahweh, marks it indelibly with the eroticism of piety's joy and utopian hope. From wilderness, springs creation and new life:

> I will make a bond for you with the animals of the fields and the birds of the air and with those that creep on the ground. I ban the bow, sword and war from the land. You will lie down in safety. Our marriage will be for ever: a betrothal in righteousness and justice, in steadfast love and in mercy. I marry you in faithfulness and you will know Yahweh. On that day, says Yahweh, I will respond to the heavens, and they to the earth and the earth will respond to the grain, the wine and the oil; and they will speak to Jezreel. I will sow myself in the land. I will have pity on 'Not-pitied'. To 'Not-my-people' I will say 'You are my people'; and he will answer: 'You are my god.'

It is clearly a mistake to see in Lamentations a contradiction to a historical account of Nehemiah's empty city. Rather, the metaphor of

Nehemiah's empty Jerusalem is reiterated in Lamentations. It is only our own historical expectations that see the image of Jerusalem as an empty and abandoned wilderness and Jerusalem as being filled with violence as contradictions. For both Nehemiah and Lamentations, as for Hosea's Jezreel in Israel, it is because of Jerusalem's sin that the desert is found; and that Mt Zion is a wasteland. I would even suggest that it is very much Lamentations' understanding of Jerusalem that lies at the heart of the Old Testament metaphor of exile. Exile is Jerusalem as a wasteland; it is the emptiness of the soul; it is to be without God. This is not historiography at all, but a metaphor of pietism. It has its roots in diaspora Judaism's self-understanding as a 'new Israel'.

Both Jeremiah, in his Lamentations over Jerusalem in the exile, and Hosea in his poems about Israel as a prostitute-wife with her bastard children, have Nehemiah's return as their points of departure. It is in an Israel redivivus that punishment, destruction and the wilderness of exile all take on meaning within the tradition. It is the 'New Jerusalem' and the Chronicler's 'New Israel' that all hold as a central theme. Collecting origin traditions about the returning 'remnant' of Israel lost, Nehemiah as origin narrative centered in rebuilding and return, *has no place* for a populated Jerusalem in his story, anymore than the book of Lamentations' poems, centered as they are in the motif of Jerusalem's repentance, has room for an Israel in Babylon. Unlike the old, lost Israel, this New Jerusalem is supersessionist: it is Israel saved, a new generation. Only those who are among the remnant who have 'turned' (in Lamentations 'repentance', and in Ezra–Nehemiah 'returned') belong. Only those whom Yahweh has changed in the wilderness, who have become again 'his people', can respond with Hosea's children: 'You are my God'. In such supersessionist logic, that is so close to the heart of the Bible's sectarian understanding of the true believer as one who has been chosen by God, the dark night of the soul (expressed biblically in the metaphor of exilic wilderness) as a time of testing and rebirth, is both a central and an essential aspect of piety's self-understanding.

We have many variants of Nehemiah's 'New Jerusalem' and Chronicles 'New Israel'. We have Ezra's renewal of the Torah and its own cluster of variations. 1 Chronicles 9's story of David's establishment of the temple service and 2 Chronicles' and Ezra's messianic Cyrus who builds a home for the God of Israel in Jerusalem, both close off the past and take a new departure for the future. We have the 'New Israels' of 1 and 2 Maccabees, the 'New Israel' of Qumran's *Damascus Covenant* as well as the post-70 generation of 'New Israels': Jamnia's and Josephus's, Mark's and Acts'. We also have New Israels implicit in each of our Old Israels: from Genesis's to Isaiah's and *Jubilees*'; from those of the psalter to Qumran's *pesherim*.

It is in texts such as Zechariah 8 that we come closest to the core of the tradition that gave rise to the concept of Israel, which structures most of the Old Testament's collections. The context is Zechariah's identification of Jerusalem as the city called Yahweh's 'holy mountain' (Zech. 8.3): 'I will save my people from the East and from the West; I will bring them home that they might live in Jerusalem, and they will be my people and I will be their God to live in faith and righteousness.' This is an ideological vision of the Old Testament that includes the wildernesses of both Nehemiah and Exodus: it is a vision stamped with the hope of a diaspora's heavenly Jerusalem.

Israel's entry into bondage in Egypt, and its return out of the desert, has variants both in Moses' vision of the desert from which Yahweh carried Israel on Eagle's wings, that we find in Deut. 32.11, and in Jeremiah's metaphor of the desert's nothingness. It is in ch. 4 that Jeremiah addresses the theme of return to a Jerusalem populated with the way of the old Israel of the destruction. 'If you return, O Israel; return to me says Yahweh. Remove your abominations from my face and do not hesitate.' Jeremiah addresses Judah and Jerusalem with the metaphor of fallow land, marking it with a theological critique of old Israel's circumcision: 'Break up the fallow ground and sow not among thorns. Circumcise yourselves to Yahweh by removing the foreskins of your hearts.' The fallow land and the desert stand as metaphorical parallels: both demanding a righteous sower. The desert wind is a wind of judgment: 'A hot wind from the barren highlands: a wilderness for the daughter of my people: it is I who speak in judgment.' Now he turns to a moral translation of the metaphor of a circumcised heart: 'Wash your heart from wickedness, that you may be saved.' Finally, it is in the stanza transition of vv. 22-23 that the desert motif of testing and judgment takes on cosmic proportions. The historiographic references to impending war and disaster demanding righteous hearts finds its summation as Yahweh addresses Jerusalem in school-masterly disdain:

> For my people are foolish; they know me not. They are stupid children; they have no understanding. They are clever at doing evil; how to do good, they know nothing of.

It is in the prophetic vision of vv. 23-26 that Jeremiah captures Jerusalem of the exile in its cosmic proportions:

> I looked on the earth; it was formless an empty: to the sky; it had no light. I looked at the mountains; they were quaking: all the hills moved back and forth. I looked; their was no human: all the birds of the air had flown. I looked; the fruitful land was a desert: its cities were laid in ruin. Before Yahweh: before his fierce anger.

In these powerful, terrible verses, the poet portrays exilic Jerusalem—this land of a people who do not know God—as an empty earth: as the world before creation. It is an image much like that of Gen. 1.1: 'When god set about to create the heavens and the earth, the earth was formless and empty and darkness was on the surface of the deep'. So, too, Jerusalem of the exile has returned in Jeremiah's vision of the desert's formlessness before God's creative and life-giving breath moved over the surface of the waters. Jerusalem is without God. It had no light; the mountains were no longer held firmly on their pillars; there was no humanity; no birds of the air. Instead of Genesis 1's divine spirit moving with its creative force, God's fierce anger governs Jeremiah's poem. It is in the face of such a wilderness Jerusalem that the poet in ch. 5 desperately searches Jerusalem's streets for a just man, that God might pardon her.

The metaphor of Israel's origins out of the desert of exile finds its creative center in the origin story of creation itself. The Genesis story brings out of the nothingness of Jeremiah's *tōhû wā-bōhû*, a wasteland which must be traversed before one comes to a new world created by God's act. This is the world of a new Jerusalem, which stands opposed to Genesis 11's Babylon's Jerusalem, with its tower built by men's hands. Does Jeremiah's metaphor evoke a new creation for his new Jerusalem? Or does the story of Genesis's creation evoke Jeremiah's metaphor of primordial chaos and place Yahweh's forgiveness of his people at the creation? Is it in the middle of such intertwining tropes that we shall ask after our historical referent so that we might know what happened? Where lies our story's referent in the creation or the exile?

The best that can be offered in answer to such a question lies outside the explicit references of our texts, outside the past of the world of tradition in which both our narratives play. It is rather in a world implicit to our texts and to our tradition as a whole. Our best answer, I

think, can be found in the confident cadences of Psalm 1 and 2's introduction to the psalter:

> Happy is...the one who has his joy in Yahweh's *torah*; who loves the
> *torah* day and night...He is like a tree who is planted on the banks of a
> canal. It will bear fruit at the right time and its leaves will not fall.
> Happy are all who find refuge in Him.

This context in piety is the historical reality that gave rise to our literary
traditions, not what they may or may not have known about the
creation, Ancient Israel or Jerusalem. The myth of exile is their myth,
not ours, and it is certainly not history's. Those who follow the way or
the advice of the ungodly, they, like the lost generation, are given over
to the desert and to death. It is this motif that is reiterated throughout
the theological metaphors of the tradition: in the murmuring stories, in
Saul's fall from grace, and in Samaria's, Jerusalem's and Babylon's
destructions. All celebrate Yahweh's cosmic victory over the ungodly
on the 'day of wrath'.

Part II

RESPONSES

THE STRANGE FEAR OF THE BIBLE:
SOME REFLECTIONS ON THE 'BIBLIOPHOBIA' IN RECENT ANCIENT ISRAELITE HISTORIOGRAPHY[1]

Hans M. Barstad

I

Several times during the discussions on 'ancient Israel' in Dublin and Lausanne objections were raised by some of the members of our Seminar whenever attempts were made to refer to historical information taken from the Hebrew Bible. Since I have always felt this to be a somewhat strange attitude for someone who claims to be a historian of Iron Age Palestine, I would like to make a few comments on this particular point of view.

Obviously, the matter in question is far too comprehensive for a short response like the present one. For this reason I shall limit myself to a few general points. I take it for granted that all the members of our Seminar (more or less) believe that knowledge of the past of some sort is possible. It is, of course, quite legitimate to be a sceptic and to deny the possibility of 'historical' knowledge altogether. However, from our discussions I did not quite get the impression that this is the case (then again I may be wrong in my assumption).

There is no need to deny that the use of the Hebrew Bible for historical (re)construction is highly uncertain (to say the least). This, however, is a problem shared by everyone who is engaged in ancient

---

1. This response was not read during any of the sessions at Lausanne. Also, it does not concern itself directly with any of the papers that were read there. Instead I have chosen to comment briefly upon one particular issue that turned up during our discussions both in Dublin and Lausanne and which, to some, appears to have become an important heuristic and methodological principle, namely, that the Hebrew Bible cannot be used as a source for any reconstruction of 'historical events' relating to the 'kingdoms' of Israel and Judah during the 'Iron Age'.

historiography.[2] My main point here must be that we cannot treat the Bible *any differently* from other historical (or rather literary) sources from the ancient world, like, for instance, those of ancient Greek or ancient Mesopotamian historiography. This is a highly important point. If someone wants to claim that the Hebrew Bible is less suitable as a basis for historical reconstruction than (say) Herodotus's *Historiae* or the 'Sumerian King List', I have no problems with this (even if I do not hold this view myself). I should, however, *need to know the grounds* for such a claim. No such grounds have sufficiently been put forward in our discussions so far. Thus, it is not enough to say that we cannot use the Bible as a historical source because it is 'unhistorical', 'unreliable', 'ideological', and so on; and moreover, that it is late (from the Hellenistic period), and that it, as a literary product far removed from the historical periods it describes, has no value for attempts to reconstruct historical reality prior to its composition.[3] All of this is something that the Hebrew Bible also shares with other ancient literary sources used for historical reconstruction. If these grounds alone should be the reason behind the claim that we cannot use the Bible for historical reconstruction, we should, consequently, have no ancient history at all. There would, in fact, be no history of ancient Egypt, of Mesopotamia, the Levant, Anatolia, Persia, Greece or Rome. Since this would represent a major upheaval in intellectual history, I believe that it is imperiously required that those scholars who plead such a special case for the cultural, compositional and cognitive status of the Hebrew Bible as compared to other ancient sources inform us why this is so. In the

---

2.   I use the word 'historiography' in two ways throughout this article: (1) stories about past events in sources used for historical reconstruction; (2) modern attempts to write 'history', that is, attempts to find out what in these same sources may be 'historically' true in a positivistic fashion.

3.   One significant problem that cannot be dealt with in this short response, but that will need considerable attention in all future discussion, concerns the question of the linguistic nature of the texts. To put it very simply: Can the Hebrew Bible be said to represent some kind of a 'linguistic museum' with a diversity bearing witness to centuries of diachronic history, or is the lack of linguistic uniformity a result of circumstances other than chronological developments? See, for instance, I. Young, *Diversity in Pre-Exilic Hebrew* (Forschungen zum Alten Testament, 5; Tübingen: J.C.B. Mohr, 1993). The most recent contribution to the debate is that of A. Hurvitz, 'The Historical Quest for "Ancient Israel" and the Linguistic Evidence of the Hebrew Bible: Some Methodological Observations', *VT* 47 (1997), pp. 301-15.

meantime we shall have to treat the Bible in a similar way as we treat other ancient literature.

II

It is not uncommon to find among orientalists and classicists who are dealing with historical issues a highly negative attitude towards the historical truthfulness of the sources with which they are working. Sometimes, this attitude goes a long way back. The reliability of Herodotus, for instance, has in varying degree been called into question ever since antiquity. At present, the (re?)discovery that the source evaluation of the 'father of history' (with its 'tripartite' ὄψις, γνώμη and ἱστορίη) has more to do with literary genres than with historical source criticism in our meaning of the word, has resulted in a heated debate over Herodotus's trustworthiness, not dissimilar to what is going on in biblical studies for the moment. The recent discussion in Greek historiography has in particular followed the publication of Detlev Fehling's *Die Quellenangaben bei Herodot* from 1971.[4] The consequence of these discussions is not that we shall have to stop using Herodotus (or other ancient sources) for historical reconstruction, but that we shall have to be even more aware of the problems we are facing when doing so. Obviously, every single piece of information will have to be examined with close scrutiny.[5]

---

4. D. Fehling, *Die Quellenangaben bei Herodot: Studien zur Erzählkunst Herodots* (Untersuchungen zur antiken Literatur und Geschichte, 9; Berlin: W. de Gruyter, 1971). See also the English translation by J.G. Howie: *Herodotus and his 'Sources': Citation, Invention and Narrative Art* (ARCA Classical and Medieval Texts, Papers and Monographs, 21; Leeds: F. Cairns, 1989). A major attack on Fehling is found in W.K. Pritchett, *The Liar School of Herodotos* (Amsterdam: J.G. Gieben, 1993). Cf. also in general the useful volume by C. Gill and T.P. Wiseman (eds.), *Lies and Fiction in the Ancient World* (Exeter: Exeter University Press, 1993).

5. For an example of how one may go about when wanting to extract historical information from Herodotus, one may compare the article by F. Thordarson ('Herodotus and the Iranians: ὄψις, ἀκοή, ψεῦδος'), the first part of which has been published in *Symbolae osloenses* 71 (1996), pp. 42-58 (I am grateful to Professor Hugo Montgomery for drawing my attention to this work). In his article Thordarson discusses the historical foundation for Herodotus's description of Scythian funeral rites in Book IV, 71-75 and demonstrates how Herodotus must have had access to genuine Scythian mythological traditions. In my view, Thordarson's work

Even if Herodotus is no doubt of great interest, and much can be learnt from studying his works,[6] ancient Near Eastern historiography must be regarded as even more relevant to historians of ancient Israel. In the present context I am thinking above all of Mesopotamian history.[7] Not only are we dealing here with literature that is closely related both from a cultural and geographical point of view, we are also dealing with a history that, for some of its periods, is closely intermingled with the history of Iron Age Palestine in a quite direct manner.

The 'Sumerian King List' may illustrate our problem. Clearly, many other texts from the vast historiographical literature of ancient Mesopotamia could have been mentioned. I have chosen the 'Sumerian King List' as an example because this is one of the texts whose historical value has been under attack. The debate is in many ways reminiscent of the discussion over the 'trustworthiness' of the Hebrew Bible.[8]

provides us with an excellent example of how to deal with the problematic field of historical reliability in ancient literary sources.

6. See, for instance, the useful survey in J. Van Seters, *In Search of History: Historiography in the Ancient World and the Origins of Biblical History* (New Haven: Yale University Press, 1984), in particular pp. 31-54. Since it has not yet appeared as I write these lines, I have not had access to the most recent contribution to this field: F.A.J. Nielsen, *The Tragedy in History: Herodotus and the Deuteronomistic History* (Copenhagen International Seminar, 4; JSOTSup, 251; Sheffield: Sheffield Academic Press, 1997).

7. The book by Van Seters, *In Search of History*, also gives a survey (pp. 55-99) of Mesopotamian historiography (Van Seters also deals in his book with other ancient Near Eastern historiographical texts). For a more complete survey of Mesopotamian historiographical texts, see A.K. Grayson, 'Assyria and Babylonia', *Or* 49 (1980), pp. 140-94. The recent, substantial volumes by A. Kuhrt, *The Ancient Near East c. 3000–330 BC, I–II* (London: Routledge, 1995), have large sections on Mesopotamian historiography. A most useful work, dealing with history of research and methodological problems, is O. Carena, *History of the Near Eastern Historiography and its Problems: 1852–1985* (AOAT, 218.1; Neukirchen–Vluyn: Neukirchener Verlag, 1989). Only the first volume (dealing with the period from 1852 to 1945) has appeared so far.

8. Nevertheless, critical Mesopotamian historiography must still be considered a field of research that is still in its very beginning. Whereas most Assyriologists are, as a rule, widely engaged with the publishing and editing of texts, they have paid less attention to the methodological, literary and ideological aspects of these texts in relation to historiography. Dealing with method are W.W. Hallo, 'Biblical History in its Near Eastern Setting: The Contextual Approach', in C.D. Evans, W.W. Hallo and J.B. White (eds.), *Scripture in Context: Essays on the Comparative Method* (PTMS, 34; Pittsburgh: The Pickwick Press, 1980), pp. 1-26; *idem*,

It is believed that the final composition of the 'Sumerian King List' took place in the late nineteenth century BCE (after the fall of the Ur III Dynasty). We are, consequently, dealing with a text that, similar to the literature of the Hebrew Bible, got its final shape considerably later than the events it describes. It is assumed that the purpose of the present form of the 'Sumerian King List' is to legitimize the rule of the kings of the Isin dynasty as the appropriate successors to the Ur III kings.[9] We are, in other words, dealing with a text that is heavily wrapped in a shroud of ideology. Also, the text is full of lacunae. Despite the many problems involved, students of early Mesopotamian history still consider the 'Sumerian King List' as a valuable source for historical information about Sumerian history. For instance, most scholars assume that the names of the kings and cities of the Agade and Ur III kings are historically correct.[10]

In the 'Sumerian King List' we have an example of a text whose status is quite similar to that of the Hebrew Bible ('late', 'ideological',

'Sumerian Historiography', in H. Tadmor and M. Weinfeld (eds.), *History, Historiography and Interpretation: Studies in Biblical and Cuneiform Literatures* (repr. Jerusalem: Magnes Press, 1984 [1983]), pp. 9-20. A rare article dealing with theory is K. Pomian, 'La reconstruction historique: point de vue réaliste', in *Historie et conscience historique dans les civilisations du Proche-Orient Ancient* (Les cahiers du CEPOA, 5; Leuven: Editions Peeters, 1989), pp. 93-107. During recent years there has been an increasing interest also in the ideological nature of Mesopotamian historiography. See F.M. Fales (ed.), *Assyrian Royal Inscriptions: New Horizons in Literary, Ideological, and Historical Analysis* (Orientis Antiqui Collectio, 17; Rome: Istituto per l'Oriente, Centro per le Antichità e la Storia dell'arte del Vicino Oriente, 1981); and F.M. Fales, 'Narrative and Ideological Variations in the Account of Sargon's Eighth Campaign', in M. Cogan and I. Eph'al (eds.), *Ah, Assyria... Studies in Assyrian History and Ancient Near Eastern Historiography Presented to Hayim Tadmor* (Scripta Hierosolymitana, 33; Jerusalem: Magnes Press, 1991), pp. 129-47.

9.   Kuhrt, *The Ancient Near East*, I, p. 77.

10.   Kuhrt, *The Ancient Near East*, I, p. 30; J.N. Postgate, *Early Mesopotamia: Society and Economy at the Dawn of History* (London: Routledge, 1992; rev. edn, 1994), pp. 28-32; H. Crawford, *Sumer and the Sumerians* (repr. Cambridge: Cambridge University Press, 1994 [1991]), pp. 19-20. Thorkild Jacobsen's suggestion that the 'Sumerian King List' also contains reliable historical information for the Early Dynastic period does, however, not have many followers today. Cf. Thorkild Jacobsen, *The Sumerian King List* (Assyriological Studies, 11; Chicago: University of Chicago Press, 1939), pp. 166-67.

'literary'), but which may still be used by historians to reconstruct historical circumstances prior to its final composition. I am not saying that this is either a good or a bad thing. The point of issue is only to claim that when scholars do use Mesopotamian literary texts for historical reconstructions, it is important that those who deny that this is possible with regard to the Hebrew Bible would also have to apply the very same procedures towards the 'Sumerian King List' (and other historiographical ancient Near Eastern sources). If not, they will most certainly have to make allowances for what it is that is so special to the Hebrew Bible that it, unlike other sources, is totally unfit for historical reconstruction. I have not seen that anything of this kind has sufficiently been done in our debate.

III

When it comes to details, each piece of information will have to be investigated separately. Here, many examples could have been mentioned. With the names of the Sumerian kings and their cities from the 'Sumerian King List' fresh in mind, it is not difficult to see here a parallel to the kings mentioned in the Deuteronomistic history. Moreover, when so many of the kings mentioned in that work (Omri, Ahab, Jehu, Joash, Ahaz, Menahem, Pekah, Hoshea, Hezekiah, Manasseh, Jehoiachin) are also referred to in sources outside the Hebrew Bible, it becomes methodologically obscure to claim that the Hebrew Bible does not yield historical information concerning periods prior to its creation. We shall, however, have to go further than that. When the historian finds that the names of all these kings are confirmed by other sources, he or she will also know something about the reliability of the Hebrew Bible, at least in this particular matter, and may also safely assume that other names of kings mentioned in the Deuteronomistic history may be historically correct.[11]

---

11. Which, of course, is precisely what many historians of ancient Israel in fact do; cf. Lester L. Grabbe, 'Are Historians of Ancient Palestine Fellow Creatures —Or Different Animals?', in *idem* (ed.), *Can a 'History of Ancient Israel' be Written?* (European Seminar in Historical Methodology, 1; JSOTSup, 245; Sheffield: Sheffield Academic Press, 1997), pp. 19-36.

I shall briefly mention just one more example. Several other, equally well-known texts could have been mentioned,[12] but the story of the last days of Judah in 2 Kings 24–25 was specifically referred to during our discussion in Lausanne. In this text we may read how Jerusalem is besieged by Nebuchadnezzar and the king, Jehoiachin, replaced by the king of Babylon with his uncle Mattaniah, who was given the name Zedekiah. Since this event is reflected also in Mesopotamian texts,[13] we have here yet another example of how the Hebrew Bible does yield reliable historical information. Again the historian, I would have thought, should say to him- or herself: This is interesting; perhaps at some time we shall have access to further extra-biblical evidence bearing witness also to other historical details found in 2 Kings 24–25. In the meantime, there is little cause not to suspect that the Hebrew Bible is correct, and that the story in 2 Kings gives us reliable information about the last days of the kingdom of Judah.[14] If one is at all interested in the historical circumstances surrounding the fall of Judah, it is very difficult to see how one can avoid using the Hebrew Bible as a historical source for the reconstruction of the history of Palestine during this particular period.

When dealing with ancient historiography, our sources will quite often have to be given the benefit of the doubt. Whether we like it or not, the pre-modern, narrative historiography of the Hebrew Bible does not provide us with verifiable historical 'facts'. Since we cannot any longer ask for historical facts the way we used to do,[15] we shall instead have to ask for what is likely (very likely, quite likely, not likely). 'Factual historical truth' must be replaced with 'narrative historical truth', which is related to 'factual truth', but not identical with it. It is, of course, always nice when historical statements are 'validated' by those of other sources. This, however, due to the very accidental nature of our sources, will always be the exception rather than the rule.

12. See the survey by F. Deist, 'The Yehud Bible: A Belated Divine Miracle?', *Journal of Northwest Semitic Languages* 23.1 (1997), pp. 117-42.

13. E.F. Weidner, 'Jojachin, König von Juda in babylonischen Keilinschriften', in *Mélanges syriens offerts à René Dussaud* (Paris: Paul Geuthner, 1939), pp. 923-35. Three different texts mention 'Jehoiachin, king of Judah'. In a fourth text he is referred to as 'the son of the king of Judah' (see pp. 925-26).

14. See the outline in L.L. Grabbe, pp. 87-88 above.

15. See my paper referred to in n. 16 below.

However, when reading some of the historiographical literature today one is left with the feeling that some scholars have made up their minds *beforehand* about the reliability of the historical information which we may find in the Hebrew Bible. Being convinced that they are 'fictitious', they are unwilling to discuss these texts in a scholarly manner. Instead, they waste a lot of energy attempting to prove what they already believe that they know. Others, again, have apparently decided beforehand that more or less everything we find in the Hebrew Bible is 'historically correct'. This other extreme, of course, must be judged as equally incompatible with the ideal of an open, scholarly mind.

IV

To conclude: As a historical source the Hebrew Bible is of the 'same' nature and quality as other ancient Near Eastern literary texts. This has the somewhat drastic consequence that if we renounce the use of the Hebrew Bible on the basis that it is late and fictional, we shall also have to do so with regard to most of the ancient sources. If we do not want to do this, we shall have to accept, for better or for worse, the Hebrew Bible not only as necessary, but also as by far the most important source for our knowledge of *the history* of Iron Age Palestine. To deny this is not only unduly hypercritical, but it is also based on a positivistic view of history that today is deplorably outdated.[16]

16. Cf. H.M. Barstad, 'History and the Hebrew Bible', in Lester L. Grabbe (ed.), *Can a 'History of Ancient Israel' be Written?* (European Seminar in Historical Methodology, 1; JSOTSup, 245; Sheffield: Sheffield Academic Press, 1997), pp. 37-64 *passim*.

EXILE? WHAT EXILE? WHOSE EXILE?

Philip R. Davies

I

In my contribution to the first of these Seminar volumes,[1] I suggested as a goal of the modern historian the pursuit of 'metahistory'—the investigation of how narratives (primary and secondary) are produced and received, and in whose interests.[2] 'The Exile' furnishes an excellent test case for such an approach, not least because 'exile' is itself a gloriously slippery term, disguising itself (to some) as representing simple historical fact or event, but clearly functioning as something different, namely, a claim about ethnicity and relationship to a 'homeland' and an implication of enforced absence. These are all far from merely claims about simple 'facts'. 'Exile' can thus be distinguished from 'diaspora' which does not necessarily carry the implication of enforcement, although Jewish mythology quite deliberately confuses the two.[3]

---

1. 'Whose History? Whose Israel? Whose Bible? Biblical Histories, Ancient and Modern', in Lester L. Grabbe (ed.), *Can a 'History of Israel' Be Written?* (European Seminar in Historical Methodology, 1; JSOTSup, 245; Sheffield: Sheffield Academic Press, 1997), pp. 104-22.

2. The role of the academic historian as critic of *ideology,* and as an investigator of how and why historiographies are generated and function, probably identifies my agenda as 'New Historicist'. For definitions and applications of this approach in the area of biblical studies of 'New Historicism', see *BibInt* 5.4 (1997), pp. 289-481. Other concerns, such as the production and reception of literary texts as inseparable from other manifestations of 'social energy' and the denial of mono-causality and periodization, are also important to the investigation of the theme of 'exile' in the Bible.

3. The Museum of the Diaspora at Tel Aviv University greets the visitor with the claim that the Jews were universally banished from their land. Here, of course, is yet another of the many examples in modern-day Israel by means of which its existence is historically and morally justified: the Yad va-Shem monument is the other. But this theme (and others), and its wider implications, has been explored

Vocabulary is, of course, crucial to any investigation of ideology, and a range of terms used in connection with population movement must be reviewed: thus 'exile' is to 'deportation' what 'migration' is to 'diaspora' (more or less), and so on.

'Exile', then, needs to be dismantled before any historical referent (ostensibly the topic of the present volume) emerges for analysis. The instigating act is a population deportation. But a population deportation, or rather population deportations from Jerusalem to Babylonia in the early sixth century BCE, emerges in the historical context of the period as one wave in an ocean of forced population movements, of which presumably only a few are recorded. It is hard to find in this particular instance any unique or distinguishing feature to justify the term '*the* Exile', and the explanation for this particular event must lie less in the peculiarities of Judaean history (though clearly these contribute) than in the mechanisms of the empires of the time.

The two moves open to the historian—an analysis of the ideological creation and an investigation of this one particular instance of an ancient pattern of population transfer—both offer plenty of scope for investigation by the historian beyond. The contributions to this volume, it seems to me, represent both lines of inquiry.

II

My own comments begin with a sketch of the ideological climate in which the modern Western historian of Israel and Judah approaches the topic. Assuming the historian to be a reader of the Bible, there are several levels at which the notion of 'the Exile' already operates upon her or him: the canonical, the literary and the historiographical. At the canonical level, the deportation brings the Former Prophets to a close: 'So Judah was carried away out of their land' (2 Kgs 25.21). Those books that deal with subsequent periods (Ezra, Nehemiah) belong elsewhere, at the end of the canon, while Chronicles is curiously displaced (after its sequel in Ezra and Nehemiah).[4] The event is thus located as a watershed, periodizing the history of the chosen people. The same

already by Norman Cantor, *The Sacred Chain: A History of the Jews* (San Francisco: HarperCollins, 1995).

4.   I am aware that there is no uniform arrangement in the traditional ordering of the Jewish scriptural canon.

effect is found at the fringes of the canon[5] (but probably not at the fringes of late Second Temple Judaism)[6] where one finds that the Exile marks an end of a sorry chapter of disobedience, while the 'postexilic' epoch extends into the present and marks the time of divine anger (as in the *Damascus Document*) or, at least, a time separately periodized into a number of years (70 by 7, as in Daniel, or 10 jubilees, as in 1 Enoch or 11QMelch) leading to the time of final divine visitation. In all cases, the 'exile' is presented as extending to the eschaton, as the present state of being. The 'exile' is thus explicitly ideological rather than geographical, and while Daniel stands as a figure, among other things, for the diaspora Jew (initiating that later equation of diaspora as Exile)[7] 'exile' defines equally the state of those Jews living in Judah. At all events, even in the Jewish scriptural canon lie the roots of that later characterization of the Jew (even the Jew in Judah) as one in exile and waiting for return, geographically and theologically.

At the literary level, too, 'the Exile' stands at the centre of a quite complex intertextual tissue. The major biblical narrative sequence that Kings brings to a close (sometimes called the 'Primary History', comprising Torah and Former Prophets) opens with a primaeval story of order out of chaos, dry land out of ocean, and follows with a tale of loss of allotted garden and banishment following human disobedience. Soon afterwards comes the Flood: judgment on the world for its wickedness, with the preservation of a small 'remnant'. These themes, regardless of any authorial or editorial intentionality, of order and chaos (mythologized as dry land and sea: or Israel and nations), of expulsion from divinely granted territory ('flowing with milk and honey', a phrase used 15 times in the Pentateuch) and of preservation of a favoured line clothe 'the Exile' with the garments of archetypal mythology. And like the great myth that it is, 'the Exile' mediates a basic contradiction: punishment and salvation. The 'exiles' are simultaneously punished for the past and by their very exile rather than destruction guaranteed salvation for the future.

5. I am thinking especially of Neh. 9.36-37 and Dan. 9.
6. See M.A. Knibb, 'The Exile in the Literature of the Intertestamental Period', *Heythrop Journal* 17 (1976), pp. 253-72.
7. It is unlikely that 'exile' characterizes the situation of diaspora Jews; to present them as such serves the interests of a Zionist ideology, both then and now: any Jew not living in the Holy Land is exiled from his proper place.

I am not here attempting any sophisticated literary analysis, nor am I insisting that every Bible reader is conscious of this patterning (indeed, even that the pattern is entirely deliberate). I am rather exposing the dimensions of influence upon the historian that a prior reading of biblical historiography is capable of exercising, underlying the way in which as literature as well as canon, the scriptural narrative as a whole creates 'the Exile' as a significant moment in the mind of the reader.

That such an influence has been exerted on modern practitioners of 'biblical history' is clear at the third level on which 'the Exile' as an *idea* can be mapped; and biblical scholarship in the twentieth century has embellished it richly. I could open my case by observing the (until recently) characteristic periodization of ancient Israelite and Judaean history into 'pre-exilic' and 'postexilic'.[8] Two further instances might be mentioned by way of example. First is the glorification of the monarchic period as the high point of 'Israelite' history, perhaps because (as Keith Whitelam has brilliantly demonstrated[9]), European scholarship saw its own nation-states mirrored in that epoch. Obviously that interest is co-opted by Zionist historians too,[10] for whom 'Israel' as an independent state is a better memory than Judah as an imperial province. Another reason for this glorification is the corresponding devaluing of the 'postexilic' period, following Wellhausen, as a time of degeneration. Whatever the fault of the monarchs, the 'pre-exilic' period at least produced prophets. The 'postexilic' period, by contrast, engendered a legalistic hierocracy that the Christian Messiah would so ringingly denounce.

A second instance of modern scholarship embellishing 'the Exile' is as a time of intellectual and theological (re)birth, through intense theological reflection and literary activity. The Priestly Code, the Pentateuch, the 'Deuteronomistic history', Isaiah 40–55 and the books of Jeremiah and Ezekiel are but the more prominent literary products

8.   The terms 'monarchic' and 'Second Temple' are tending to replace this terminology. 'Monarchic' is an entirely unobjectionable term; 'Second Temple', however, much less so, since we actually have no evidence that this period embraced the history of only the second Judaean temple in Jerusalem, nor of a single temple at that. It is a term already laden with (biblically based) ideology.

9.   Keith W. Whitelam, *The Invention of Ancient Israel: The Silencing of Palestinian History* (London: Routledge, 1996).

10.   In the present overheated political climate it is important to reiterate that 'Zionist' does not equate to either 'Jewish' or 'Israeli'.

assigned by a majority of recent (though increasingly fewer) scholars to a period and place in the sixth century of which we know very little (even from the canonized literature).[11] To some extent this move is dictated by a penchant for the earliest possible dating of a piece of canonized writing (an instinct among many biblical historians of this century) for literature that bears a clear stamp of post-monarchic production.

Additionally, a certain romanticism should perhaps not be excluded as a factor in the scholarly reconstruction of 'the Exile'. The idea that in the punishment of exile a chastened 'Israel' reflected on its own past sins and prepared itself for restoration is an example of one of the powerful mythical *topoi* of Western Christian culture: the fallen sinner, through repentance, reflects upon past misdeeds and, duly forgiven and renewed, is liberated to a new life as a new being. Only suffering can bear great theological fruit!

III

These comments, by no means adequate let alone exhaustive, are intended to demonstrate the thesis that 'the Exile' is clouded in an ideological mist, that it comes to any modern interpreter pre-interpreted and with mythical rather than legendary dressing.

But this is only half of my thesis; for my concern is also with the realia (I leave the term for the moment unproblematized), for without some knowledge of the events that constitute the wellspring of 'the Exile' we cannot totally explain the mythical configurations. The agenda I am pursuing does not by any means minimize the importance of historical events, for every myth and every idea, every ideological construction has, according to my materialist philosophy,[12] a basis in human political, social and economic life.

---

11. Ironically, it is from such scholars that one hears criticisms of proposals to date much of this literature to the Persian period, on the grounds that we know virtually nothing of this period. The same is true of the 'exilic' period (except that the qualification 'virtually' is unnecessary).

12. I assume a materialist approach to be more or less agreed by those who are interested in biblical history as well as biblical archaeology, the assumption being that the historical and cultural configurations in some way clarify the ideological products. However, there remains a very strong idealist strand in much biblical scholarship, deriving either from Western philosophical roots or (more probably) from theistic beliefs. Biblical history as a discipline has always been methodologically weak, but philosophically perhaps even weaker, and a debate about the

The historical events that undergird 'the Exile' are, first, a series of deportations and emigrations from Judah early in the sixth century BCE, namely, enforced transportation to Babylonia and voluntary flight to Egypt.[13] Then, no less important, there is also indirect but persuasive evidence of immigration into Judah, both from neighbouring territories and from Babylonia, and, again, as both voluntary and coercive.[14] These movements correspond to what biblical scholars call 'the Return' (or formerly 'the Restoration') and produce the claim on the part of the immigrants to have been exiles. The details of these population movements are analysed elsewhere in this volume and there is no need to rehearse them: the point I make is simply that we are dealing essentially with two directions of population movement, which the historian should accept as having occurred. How much further can this historian go towards endorsing 'the Exile'?

Here one reaches an obstacle. For is that there can be *no* historical event or events corresponding in a simple or direct way to 'the Exile', largely (but not entirely) because 'exile' is in any case not that kind of a thing? 'Exile' is already an interpretation. It interprets those 'exiled' as belonging to a piece of land, and indeed constructs that piece of land as belonging to them (and implicitly to no one else, including present inhabitants); it also interprets the land as definitive of identity, for an assimilated exile ceases to be an exile, though without necessarily losing all ethnic affiliation. The point is made fully elsewhere in this volume by the Irishman Robert Carroll.

What, if anything, would make 'the Exile' into a part of the history of Judah? This can be answered, theoretically at least: a demonstration (a) that the bulk of the population of Judah was forcibly separated from the land it regarded as its own; (b) of the persistence of a consciousness on the part of that population that it 'belonged' to the former land and not to its present habitat; and (c) that the population was restrained from returning to the land claimed as its own. The first and last of these

philosophical assumptions underlying modern approaches to the history of ancient Israel and Judah is long overdue.

13. The direct evidence for such a flight is confined to the canonized narrative (2 Kgs 25.26, etc.), but the presence of large numbers of Jews in Egypt in subsequent periods may support this, although migration from Palestine to Egypt has been continuous throughout recorded history.

14. Whether any of the transfers under the Persians was coercive is hard to say for certain, but it is by no means unlikely.

are capable of determination by a historian, and perhaps the second might be reasonably established. But one important factor is the passage of time. For over a certain period (we will not try to specify), several things occur: the departed homeland becomes the home of others, so that 'exile' is constructed as a contested political claim; and those regarding themselves as in 'exile' come to belong also to their new place of residence, and this consciousness of belonging to the new place erodes the strength of the claim to belong elsewhere and thus to be in exile. Indeed, it might be questioned how far the child of an exile born to a deportee in the place of exile can be called an exile. I do not seek to answer this, merely to point out that even when attempting to be 'objective', the historian is drawn into judgments about matters that go well beyond 'facts' and 'events'. 'Exile', as I have already said, quickly becomes a political word and its capacity for neutral description is quickly reduced to zero.

Here I want to interject briefly. My own claim, as a Welshman, to feel exiled from the homeland of my ancestors (I can choose virtually the whole of Britain, for were my ancestors not the 'Britons', unlike the later Anglo-Saxon and Norse invaders?) is justified by the forced expulsion of my ancestors, but weakened by the passing of many centuries. In that sense any claim on my part to be an exile from England would now appear ridiculous, and I instantly disqualify myself.

But I did move to England, to this homeland that I *might* have ridiculously claimed. I now live in England and have done so for most of my life. I am, in fact, in a much better position to claim exile from Wales than exile from ancient Britain (the term 'exile' is often applied to the Welsh in England, when 'Mafia' is not preferred). But since my parents were not forced from Wales and nothing prevents me from returning to live there, I am not an exile from Wales, either. I am at best an *émigré*. Introducing my own case (a rather more complicated one than Robert Carroll's, though as an Irishman he now lives in a country once colonized by Irish peoples known as 'Scots'...) is meant, nevertheless intended not as a piece of fashionable autobiographical criticism, but as an illustration of the slipperiness of the term 'exile'. I could add that my own situation entitles me personally as well as morally to discuss 'exile' when applied to other peoples, and perhaps even more so when it comes to being colonized, of which both the Welsh and the Irish know a good deal.[15] But at all events, I disqualify myself from being able to claim exilic status either from England or from Wales. I am simply an economic migrant.

I now return to the biblical 'Exile'. In this case we also have to confront the existence of other Judaean populations that also have to be called 'Judah' and continue to live in that territory; and also the descendants of erstwhile Judaean deportees in Babylonia who clearly transferred their homeland to Babylonia by the expedient of choosing to remain there. The existence of these populations relativizes the description 'exile' to a certain population, potentially recognized among a group that return to the claimed homeland when permitted to do so. Thus they cease to be exiles, of course, and simultaneously disqualify non-returnees as any longer 'exiles' because these have now definitively elected a new homeland. The act of returning also constitutes, actually or potentially, a claim against existing residents. In the canonized narrative, the term 'exile' is justified by a story in which all of Judah disappear, so that there remain no legitimate alternative claimants to the land itself. 2 Kgs 25.12 mentions the 'poor of the land', but either v. 26 means to imply that these also leave or, as 'poor' they do not actually *possess* any of the land itself and so do not count merely on the pretext of being there.[16] A population visible to the modern historian is either invisible or transparent in the literature of the immigrants. Equally visible to the historian but invisible or transparent in the canonized narrative (though eminently visible elsewhere in canonized literature, in Esther, Daniel or Tobit) are those descendants of deportees who took the ethnic affiliation 'Judaean/Jew' but did not return to Judah even when restraints were removed, but remained in Mesopotamia or elsewhere. Probably (but not necessarily) these formed the origins of substantial Jewish populations there centuries later.

The immigrants, then, appropriated to themselves exclusively the identities of 'Judah' (and/or 'Israel'), silencing both the other groups. The silencing was achieved literarily, but also politically; the historian can observe the former but only deduce the latter. Ideologically the

15. This may explain my sensitivity to the plight of modern colonized (by Turks, British, now Israelis) Palestinians. But as will shortly be seen, the issue of colonizing also belongs in this discussion of 'the Exile' and so I confront as a historian the issue of colonization in ancient Judah (part of Palestine).

16. This is perhaps speculative, but the same argument is used in the same part of the world today.

displacement by 'exiles' of 'non-exiles' was achieved by asserting the following propositions: (a) monarchic Judah was punished by banishment from its land by its deity, and so non-banishment meant non-membership of the nation; (b) those left behind had been mixed with other racial groups and had abandoned the ethnic practices of Judah (so Ezekiel, Ezra, Nehemiah); (c) the land was in fact empty anyway, and had to be because it also needed rest from its previous pollution (2 Chron. 36.21, etc.).

It is thus possible for the historian to speak of a group using 'Exile' as a political claim, but not to identify these as 'Judah' or 'the Jews', but only one of several groups entitled to that claim, yet for whom 'exile' was not an experience. In other words, the historian can identify whose *story the 'Exile' belongs to*, and point to a group (or a cluster of groups) which will have been in contest over its claims as Judah with at least one other group (or groups). 'Exile' is not an episode in the 'history of Israel'; it is an ideological claim on behalf of a certain population element in the province of Judah during the Persian period. From this basis, the historian can see the history of this claim to modern times; can discern how it has successfully achieved its own aim of defining both 'Judah' and 'Israel' on its own terms. That success, of course, has been achieved largely through the production of a historiography (and other forms of literature) that have become canonized in Christianity as well as in Judaism, and so have gained a historical authority that they would not otherwise have (and do not, of course, deserve).

But we are currently on another path, inspecting the claim made on behalf of these groups actually to have been 'returned exiles'. While I retain a strong attachment to such an investigation, I am dubious about the possibility of success. First, we cannot know what these people thought about themselves at the moment of return, as opposed to what their literature reflects. Did they believe they were descendants of Judaeans deported several generations ago? Even if we could answer this in the affirmative, we then need to know whether they were mistaken, and indeed, what would count as a 'mistake', for ethnicity is not necessarily a matter of pure genealogy. Clearly it is *one* of the criteria, indeed the chief criterion, used in Ezra and Nehemiah (and elsewhere in the canonized writings) to define who is Judaean and who is not. But it is well known that this biological definition functions as a social and political code and not a scientific claim about genes. We know that ethnicity equates to neither linear descent nor to culture.[17] In some sense, the immigrants constructed themselves as exiles, enforced their identity as Judaeans, and became Judaeans. To wonder whether this claim was originally technically justified is not only impossible, but also rather inconsequential.

IV

'Exile' is the ideological means by which such an act is justified. The Deuteronomic presentation of the monarchies of Judah and Israel precisely undergirds the claim of those from Babylonia to be the real Israel, by identifying their 'exile' as a punishment on Israel from Israel's deity. The genealogical argument was also used in defence of racial purity and in imputing intermarriage to non-'exiles'. The argument was powerful enough (because backed by political and perhaps military force) to override any claims the remaining population may have had to consider themselves the heirs of the older monarchic Judah, and the canonization of the claim has persuaded modern so-called historians to adopt the idea as a historical datum, tracing the history of 'Israel' through deportation and back into Judah, and speaking of 'restoration'.

For the historian interested in the negotiation of power, this particular 'exile' belongs to the discourse of colonization. Focus on the reality of the relevant deportation(s) is important, of course, in countering the claim that it was 'Judah' that was transported, and in asking instead who, why and when was removed, as well as who was left behind. But what makes this 'exile' unique is not yet another imperial deportation from a tiny kingdom to the metropolitan centre, but the canonized story of a group claiming to be 'exiles' and successfully defining themselves as the continuation of monarchic Judah (and monarchic Israel). Whether in fact that claim makes sense *on the terms that the narrative*

---

17. See the excellent recent survey of this whole question by S. Jones, *The Archaeology of Ethnicity: Constructing Identities in the Past and Present* (London: Routledge, 1997). The confusion of culture and ethnicity, incidentally, is still perpetuated in biblical studies and biblical archaeology, as the current debate about the origins of Israel demonstrates. See the altercation between Whitelam (who understands the difference) and Dever (who does not) in *JSOT* 72 (1996): William G. Dever, 'The Identity of Early Israel: A Rejoinder to Keith W. Whitelam', pp. 3-24; and Keith W. Whitelam, 'Prophetic Conflict in Israelite History: Taking Sides with William G. Dever', pp. 25-44.

presents is an important question, to which I and others have answered firmly in the negative. The picture of monarchic Israel and Judah in the canonized literature is an essentially fictional retrojection. (I suppose I need again to underline that this does not amount to a denial that either a kingdom of Israel or a kingdom of Judah existed, nor an assertion that the contents of the canonized narratives are entirely invented. The most helpful analogy is with historical fiction, in which historical characters do unhistorical things, unhistorical characters do historical things and unhistorical characters do unhistorical things.)

But to insist on the canonized history of ancient Judah being rejected as the basis for a critical history does not mean rejecting a history of Judah. Indeed, the fact is that the 'exiles' are the historical successors of the monarchy of Judah in terms of geographical and political continuity. Indeed, they belong not only to the history of the land but to the history of the term 'Judaean'. Their heritage is a simple matter of fact. It was for them important to legitimate that succession; for the modern historian such a succession is already a matter of record and needs no legitimating. Consequently, arguments about the rightness of the claims made are of little importance.

Little importance, indeed, to the historian *qua* ancient historian. But the narratives with which this historian deals are canonized; and they also function as legitimation for modern instances of colonization. It is for that reason that modern biblical historians, even more so than most other modern historians of the ancient world, find themselves time and again challenging and confronting each other, becoming embroiled in angry disputes of the sort that to an uninformed outsider would seem to be unjustified by the inconsequentiality of the issues. Debate about 'the Exile', like so much 'biblical history' is not entirely about ancient history after all.

EXILE A PERIOD—EXILE A MYTH

Knud Jeppesen

In a recent article in *Nordisk Judaistik*,[1] the phrase *den judiska exilen* (the Jewish exile) is used in the title and elsewhere to designate the life of the Jewish community in Sweden before, during and after the Second World War. The article is a review of discussions in a Jewish periodical, *Judisk Tidsskrift*, about the problem of whether all Jews should end the exile and choose freedom in Palestine, or whether some of them could still have a meaningful Jewish existence in a diaspora.[2]

This article in Swedish is only one among many examples in the literature, showing that 'exile' is used about the continuing history of the Jews outside their original country, even in cases where the word 'diaspora' seems to have been the right expression.[3] For biblical scholars, however, 'the exile' normally designates a specific period in Israel's history in the sixth century BCE. Scholars debate the dates for the two ends, but still this period is normally supposed to have both a beginning and an end.

On top of these two meanings of exile, the completed and the not completed, and in some way related to both meanings, 'exile' is used as

---

1.   Anders Englund, 'Den nya juden och judiska exilen i Judisk Tidsskrift 1933–1950', *Nordisk Judaistik (Scandinavian Jewish Studies)* 17.1-2 (1996), pp. 1-23.

2.   The author does not make a point of it, but it seems from the article that the spokesmen for the gathering of the Jews in Palestine used the word *exile*, while the Jews who thought it possible still to live a Jewish life in Sweden (for example), even after the establishment of the modern state Israel, preferred the Swedish word *förskingringen*, the equivalent of diaspora. Indirectly this shows that the word 'exile', used about the situation in the twentieth century, is more coloured by political ideology than 'diaspora' seems to be.

3.   Cf. L.L. Grabbe's remark in his contribution that the terminology 'diaspora' is better than 'exile', when we talk about Jewish congregations outside Judah in the Second Temple period (p. 90 above).

a strong religious and philosophical metaphor about a catastrophe which in the end it was possible to come through.

The papers in the present volume discuss first and foremost 'exile' in two meanings—a period in Israel's history and a metaphor—and the mutual relation between these two meanings. The contributions by R. Albertz, B. Becking, and L.L. Grabbe deal primarily with the problem of whether and how much we are able to reconstruct the history of the period,[4] but they also have an eye for the symbolic meaning of exile. T. Thompson and R.P. Carroll, on the other hand, are much more inclined to explore the myth of exile in their papers, and especially Thompson rejects a connection of 'exile' specifically with the sixth-century BCE period.

In the following few pages I want to comment upon two points raised by these papers. The first is related to the history of research into Israel's history; the other has to do with myth and history, especially, of course, in relation to exile as a period and exile as a myth.

I

The period known as the 'exile' is one of the areas where the research into the history of Israel started. As stressed several times in the above-mentioned papers, there is no biblical narrative about the exile to take as the point of departure for a description of the period.

As long as scholars believed that what earlier was called in German scholarship *das große Religionsbuch* (Genesis to 2 Kings[5]) was primarily a history book, they felt that they could make what Barstad has termed 'a *paraphrastic recapitulation* of the biblical stories'[6] and tell the recapitulation as the history of this period.

But a paraphrastic recapitulation can only be made until the fall of Jerusalem; as is well known, 'das große Religionsbuch' ends where the exile starts. Therefore, any scholar who wants to write a history of the

4.   In the seminar discussion Hans M. Barstad's book, *The Myth of the Empty Land: A Study in the History and Archaeology of Judah during the 'Exilic' Period* (Symbolae osloenses, 28; Oslo: Scandinavian University Press, 1996), was also taken into consideration. Barstad's interest is 'concerned primarily with the question of what was actually going on in Judah during the period commonly referred to as the "Exile"' (p. 23).

5.   This designation is found in, e.g., B. Duhm, *Das Buch Jesaia* (HAT, 3.1; Göttingen: Vandenhoeck & Ruprecht, 1892), p. v.

6.   Barstad, *The Myth of the Empty Land*, p. 26 (emphasis mine).

Israelites from Abraham to the Maccabees has to present some kind of reconstruction when she or he goes beyond Nebuchanezzar's conquest and destruction of Jerusalem. There is not *one* history, which can be supposed to be *the* history after 587–586 BCE.

Even the most conservative scholars, who generally are convinced that all information in the Bible is historically correct, have to make a reconstruction of the exilic history. And reconstructions will always have a subjective touch because there are choices to be made between different biblical and other information.

The need for reconstruction is also well documented in the papers in this volume. But until recently this has not been felt to be a major problem. In the textbooks statements like the following are found:

> Die Lücke zwischen der Erzählung über die Exilierung am Ende der Königsbücher und dem Parallelbericht von Jer 52 sowie dem Schluß der Chronikbücher einerseits und den Mitteilungen über die Rückkehr aus dem Exil im chr Esrabuch anderseits läßt sich jedoch *unschwer* einigermaßen ausfüllen.[7]

An important point in the research represented in this book is that nobody should use the term *unschwer* (not difficult) in this connection any more. Albertz, who does not want to be a 'minimalist', is forced to be so in this context. His first sentence reveals it: 'Die Exilzeit stellt in der biblischen Gesichtsdarstellung ein finsteres Loch dar' ('The exile period represents a black hole in the biblical historical narrative'), and later on he admits that the exile is 'a black box', in which scholars place what they cannot believe belongs to the pre-exilic period.

But in the end Albertz tries to reconstruct some features of the history in question by means of external sources; Becking ends up after a discussion about the contents of the book of Ezra still being convinced that 'processes like "exile" and "return" have taken place'—but we know too little; and Grabbe, after investigations into both biblical and extra-biblical material, comes to the conclusion: 'The biblical concept of exile and return was, therefore, based on actual events.'

---

7. 'The gap between the story about the beginning of the exile at the end of the books of Kings, and the parallel report in Jer. 52 as well as the end of Chronicles on the one hand and the notices about the return from exile in the chronicler's book of Ezra on the other, is not difficult to fill in reasonably after all.' A.H.J. Gunneweg, *Geschichte Israels bis Bar Kochba* (Theologische Wissenschaft, 2; Stuttgart: W. Kohlhammer, 5th edn, 1984), p. 126 (emphasis mine).

When a piece of history is reconstructed there will always be details to discuss; but I do not intend to take this discussion up here. I agree in principle with scholars like Albertz, Becking and Grabbe, about the idea that we still have some 'exile' story to tell, especially a story around 587–586 BCE.

As pointed out in some of the contributions above there have been several exiles (or maybe better 'deportations') of people in the Old Testament. But still, when we talk about *the* exile both as a historical period and as a myth, this has something to do with events that happened in the sixth century BCE, beginning with the fall of Jerusalem and the destruction of the temple. These are events where history and myth meet.

Admittedly, there are very few 'pivots' on which we can place our story—but it is no problem if it turns out to be a very short story which some will call minimalistic. And there are, of course, lots of issues that we cannot solve today and we probably never will be able to solve.

One of the problems that comes up again and again in this book is the relation or continuity between the group, which went out from Jerusalem and its surroundings 'before the exile', and the group which went into Jerusalem and its surroundings 'after the exile'.[8] But I cannot see that this unsolved problem necessarily prevents us from telling the exile's history; and we have to deal with the 'return', too, because the return is where the story about the completed exile and the not-completed exile meet. The unended exile gets its hope from the history and the myth concerning the ended exile, which began in 597–596 BCE. It is from this point onward that we—with Carroll—can say 'Yes!' as well as 'No!' to the question of whether the exile ever ended.

It is difficult to be absolutely sure whether or not the story we can tell is the historically true story about the period in question, but this may not be so important after all. Any historical account—no matter how much secure evidence we use to make it—has traces of a reconstruction that is not at all unique to the history of the 'exile'. And being a reconstruction it is in the end the creation of the author; as soon as we *tell* the story, it becomes more or less a 'bogus history' (Carroll); we cannot avoid that—and I don't think we should try to avoid it.

---

8.   Maybe even the terminology pre- and postexilic is wrong; cf. Carroll's quotations from C.C. Torrey, *Ezra Studies* (Chicago: University of Chicago Press, 1910), pp. 287-88.

On the contrary, we shall continue to tell history, even if we don't always know when we get to the point where we ought to put the word in inverted commas. We have to take into consideration that when we have used the scientific tools thoroughly, when we have found the available historical details, in a way we have moved from science to art—not always fine art of course! But *telling* the history as a narrative is more 'art' than it is 'science'. But if we want to share our results with others, we have to place the results into a continuous story, the story we call 'history'. This has always been the case and will always be the case—and this has nothing to do with the problem of whether we can use the Bible as a historical source or not.

II

Brought up as I am with Scandinavian traditio-history, I was given the impression, when I first studied the Old Testament as a university subject, that the people who were taken away from Jerusalem after the conquest had had experiences which were so serious and deep that a myth was needed if they were to survive. I was taught that the Judaeans overcame the exile, because they knew the only myth that was able to interpret the suffering and to promise hope for a better future: the myth of death and resurrection.

On this background I am, of course, very much familiar with and in favour of the idea expressed in different ways in these papers, that *exile* is myth, metaphor, symbol, or even a black box. Today, however, I would probably put my arguments in a different order than I first learnt to put them; we cannot know whether the Judaeans were saved because they knew a myth, or whether they invented a myth themselves or applied a well-known myth to their situation because and after they were saved. What we know is that there are texts which reveal that people in exile or after an exile has ended were able to give words to their experiences by using the myth of death and resurrection.

Maybe I have given up much of what I learnt in the Scandinavian school, but I still believe in the basic concept that the exile is interpreted in the Bible as an aspect of a universal myth. I therefore appreciate Carroll's and Thompson's attempt simply to understand the exile as a myth, if not *the* myth, that is, the basic religious message that there is no disaster so serious that you cannot escape it, if God so wills.

But still, as already stressed, I think that there is some kind of connection between the exile in history and the exile in the mythical narrative. You can say that all texts about the exile are nothing else than reflections of the myth, but there are still events, which were part of the process where the understanding was made deeper, or as said above, where the history and the myth meet.

Barstad rightly points out: 'The *ideological* "exile", which formed a natural part of the biblical tradition, later became an inherent part of our scholarly *historical* tradition, from which we now are having great difficulties freeing ourselves.'[9] He here points to a wrong development in the Old Testament research, no doubt about that. The ideology—the myth—and the narrative—the 'history'—are two different ways of recognition which we have to distinguish from each other. Scholars often mix them, and therefore it is difficult for myth and history to live peacefully together. We need both of them, but we must draw a dividing line between them.

This line must not, on the other hand, be so impenetrable that we cannot put questions from the myth to history or vice versa. Thompson blames Barstad for asking 'literary questions' of archaeology; but will the questions we ask of archaeology not always be 'literary' in some way or other? Literature is our background, and the curiosity that makes scholars dig exists because somebody has read texts. It might be wrong to ask archaeology about the reliability of some texts we have read; on the other hand, the question about reliability is such a good question, why not ask it—even when we know for certain that the answer we can get will always be tentative (cf. Becking)?

To conclude, I don't find it necessary to choose between myth and history, as long as we don't mix them up. For biblical scholars a choice between myth and history is equivalent to a choice between history and the Bible. If that were the choice, I would always prefer the Bible—it is much more exciting than history.

9.   Barstad, *The Myth of the Empty Land*, p. 22.

Part III

CONCLUSIONS

REFLECTIONS ON THE DISCUSSION

Lester L. Grabbe

The focus on 'the exile' for the 1997 discussion turned out to be a very beneficial exercise. It provided a concentration on issues which helped to clarify the agreements and disagreements among the Seminar members and the different approaches to the same subject when all were drawing on the same limited data. In addition, it brought to the surface some of the main methodological issues which also seem to be important for the history of 'Israel'[1] in the centuries prior to the Neo-Babylonian period. In the summary that follows, I draw on both the papers and responses printed in this volume and on the discussion in the meeting of the Seminar. In order to differentiate between the two, I use the full surname to refer to the individual papers and responses prepared for the Seminar.[2] When I refer to comments in the discussion, I refer to Seminar participants only by initials.[3]

---

1. I use the term in quote marks because of the moot question of whether there was ever a united kingdom or whether the term 'Israel' should be applied jointly to both the Northern and Southern Kingdoms. For the problems involved in the use of various terminology, see the remarks of different contributors to Lester L. Grabbe (ed.), *Can a 'History of Israel' Be Written?* (European Seminar in Historical Methodology, 1; JSOTSup, 245; Sheffield: Sheffield Academic Press, 1997), especially pp. 12-13, 65-66, 129-38, 150-55, 188-89.

2. The recent book by Hans M. Barstad, *The Myth of the Empty Land: A Study in the History and Archaeology of Judah During the 'Exilic' Period* (Symbolae osloenses, 28; Oslo: Scandinavian University Press, 1996), will also be referred to at various points, but this will always be done via footnotes.

3. The following initials are used:

RA	Rainer Albertz	LLG	Lester L. Grabbe
BB	Bob Becking	KJ	Knud Jeppesen
HMB	Hans M. Barstad	EAK	E. Axel Knauf
RPC	Robert P. Carroll	NPL	Niels Peter Lemche
PRD	Philip R. Davies	TLT	Thomas L. Thompson

Given the diverse make-up of the Seminar there were two remarkable agreements that encompassed everyone who participated. The first was that one or more deportations from both the Northern and Southern Kingdoms had indeed occurred. No one questioned this fact. The second was that 'the exile' is a term heavily loaded with theological and ideological significance and thus not a neutral designation of a mere historical period or episode. No one doubted that use of the term necessarily evoked images not only relating to Neo-Babylonian history but also to the Jewish interpretation of the past and even the identity and self-image of the Jewish people both historically and in the present. The discussion and debate on the topic was done in the context of these perceptions which all had in common.

Use of the Term 'The Exile'

The theological and ideological overtones of the term 'exile/the exile' was touched on in most of the papers. The one to explore the topic most thoroughly was Carroll, followed by Thompson and Davies, but they were by no means the only ones to say something at some length on the subject. The main question introduced for Seminar discussion was whether the term 'the exile' should be dropped from scholarly usage because of the inevitable theological baggage coming with it whenever it is used. In contrast to most other issues, members of the Seminar were fairly sharply divided into two clear groups on this one issue.

Some felt that the term was too problematic to use, noting that it was simply a taking over of the biblical agenda (NPL) whereas different language needed to be used to avoid misunderstandings and clouding of the issue (TLT). Since there was no deportation of most of the inhabitants of Judah, most did not experience exile; for those who did, there was no end to that exile (and thus no 'restoration') because most did not return to the land (PRD). To continue to use 'exile' is as problematic as continuing to use 'patriarchal period' (NPL). There was no Israel of which exile and return was a part of its history (PRD), since no inhabitants of the Northern Kingdom are anywhere alleged to have returned.

Others accepted that 'exile' or 'exile/return' was in some sense a correct description since some people had been exiles and some of their descendants had returned (EAK); despite the theological overtones it was a conventional term and well understood in scholarship (HMB, BB). If one is talking in the context of the 'history of Israel', then the term might as well be used rather than engaging in a fruitless debate (RA). The important thing is to define the content of what is intended by the term (EAK). Use of 'the exile' is not in the same category as 'patriarchal period' (BB) since the former was not a purely theological construct as is the latter.

One suggestion about finding a neutral term was that one might speak of 'deportation' instead of 'exile' (PRD). Everyone agreed that there had a been a deportation—in fact, many deportations—during this period. This met with some favour and was also sometimes used in some of the papers as an attempt to get away from the word 'exile'. On the other hand, it was objected that this too was following the biblical agenda (NPL).

It was clear that no agreement was likely on this issue, and this portion of the debate was quickly brought to an end. Some will continue to use 'exile' and 'exile and restoration' despite their problematic nature, and the terms 'pre-exilic' and 'postexilic' as shorthand for purely chronological indications are hard to get away from. It is hoped that such usage will be defined or clarified as needed in the individual context. Others will continue to try to find a more neutral designation for the deportations which no one doubts took place.

Return of Deportees and the Question of Continuity with the Pre-Deportation Community

The expression 'exile/return' is so often spoken of and used that the questions begged seem never to be discussed or addressed. A person, group or community can go into exile and can then return after a period of time. Yet this is not what is proposed in the case of either those deported from Samaria in the late eighth century or from Judah in the early sixth century. Although there are a few examples of genuine return from exile recorded from elsewhere in the ancient Near East (Grabbe), no one has argued that those taken out of the Palestinian region returned. Thompson has especially emphasized this lack of continuity and has inferred from it that one cannot therefore speak of a 'return from exile' in the case of the Judaeans in the Persian period. People who came into the land in a later period created the idea by claiming to be descendants of those deported, yet the supposed return could just be another deportation (TLT). Other peoples were brought in to replace those taken out. This further illustrates the terminological difficulties and the need to be explicit and precise about what is being proposed.

Nevertheless, some felt that even though the original deportees did not return, there was still a sufficient continuity to speak of a 'return from exile'. One aspect of this debate concerns the nature of continuity and how to evaluate it. Is it sufficient to call it a 'return' or 'restoration' if the descendants of the original deportees return? There is, after all, what might be called 'biological continuity'. However, there is agreement that the descendants of the original deportees as a whole did not return, only a portion. The community created by the deportation continued to exist, and only a minority of its constituents returned by any reckoning. If most of the original community was left in the land and not deported, and if most of the descendents of those deported did not return to the original homeland, how accurate is it to speak of 'the return'? Particularly, how accurate it is to speak of a 'restoration'?[4] We once again get into the territory of whether we should use conventional terminology even if it is not strictly accurate. There would probably be less objection to 'return', which at least would not be wholly inaccurate, than to 'restoration' which is more problematic.

What if there is no *biological* continuity, though? What if a group of people is brought into the land and has or takes on the culture, literature and mythology of those who were deported? Is this sufficient continuity to speak of a 'return from exile', even if a strict biological relationship cannot be proved? To put it another way, can you dismiss the claims of those who label themselves 'returnees from exile' when this could be only the claims of another people deported from their original homeland (TLT)? NPL draws attention to a modern definition of ethnicity which says that an ethnic group consists of people who think of themselves as belonging to this group and are seen as members of it by nonmembers. Biology is not important, only the idea of being part of the community. In spite of its own ideology, an ethnic group is comprised

---

4. Although Barstad (*The Myth of the Empty Land*) does not explicitly discuss the validity of using the term 'restoration', both his and Robert Carroll's 'The Myth of the Empty Land', in David Jobling and Tina Pippin (eds.), *Ideological Criticism of Biblical Texts* (Semeia, 59; Atlanta: Scholars Press, 1992), pp. 79-93, studies show the problematic nature of the biblical picture.

of people who have for whatever reason been accepted by the group as members. Genealogical manipulation takes care of the supposed biological connection. Although there may not be any biological descendants of those deported among the returnees, this is not important if they belong to a group which identifies itself as that which was deported. Among the population of Denmark are descendants of Tartars who settled there 300 years ago. They think of themselves as Danes and consider the history of Denmark in the past thousand years and more as *their* history, even if they may also remember that they have another, different past.

The Samaritan community is a good example to illustrate the debate over the significance of biological continuity. Their own self-understanding is that they were descended from the Northern Kingdom (though they also claim to have been taken into exile and then been allowed to return[5]), whereas the Jewish claim was that they were foreigners brought in who simply adopted some of the Israelite customs and a form of its religion. This example also shows that the debate over 'exile and return' is not a recent one but instead has a long history.

If recent estimates are anywhere near correct, millions of people were deported from their homelands to be settled elsewhere during the Neo-Assyrian, Neo-Babylonian and Persian periods.[6] This enormous mixing up of the people has been emphasized, with its consequences for any continuity of identity and ethnicity (Thompson). The loss of national or ethnic identity seems to have taken place with those deported from the Northern Kingdom in 722 BCE, yet it was not invariable that a resettled community lost its bond with the original homeland. Examples are known of groups who retained the identity of their original place of settlement centuries after being removed and resettled (Grabbe). Therefore, one cannot make a blanket statement about what would happen to a deported community since either retention or loss of identity is possible, but it at least allows the possibility that the descendants of a deported community who settle in the original homeland would see themselves as an example of 'exile and return'. The length of time since the original deportation is a significant factor since there

5. For details, see L.L. Grabbe, 'Betwixt and Between: The Samaritans in the Hasmonean Period', in E.H. Lovering, Jr (ed.), *Society of Biblical Literature 1993 Seminar Papers* (SBLSP, 32; Atlanta: Scholars Press, 1993), pp. 334-47.

6. Bustenay Oded, *Mass Deportations and Deportees in the Neo-Assyrian Empire* (Wiesbaden: Reichert, 1979), pp. 19-22.

is always some change, even if the period is short (BB).

The Self-Understanding of Those in the 'Diaspora'

The question of self-understanding and self-identity can be a touchy subject, as Robert Carroll noted both in his paper and in the discussion. For example, many descendants of Irish immigrants retain a strong identity with Ireland, and Irish-Americans provide the main financial backing for various of the paramilitary groups in Northern Ireland. Yet they regard America as their home and would not seriously contemplate moving back to Ireland. Philip Davies draws on his Welsh origins to note an attachment to the place of origin but in fact to live elsewhere voluntarily. One can think of 'tax exiles' and all sorts of others who choose to live outside their country of birth even though they remain citizens of it. Knud Jeppesen points to the debate (before the founding of the state of Israel) in Sweden between Jews who saw themselves as Swedish citizens first and as Jews only second, and those who thought that their first loyalty should be to a Jewish homeland. A similar situation pertained in Denmark where there were no 'Jews' as such, only Danes with a Jewish religion; this is why they were treated differently in Denmark from elsewhere in Europe (NPL). This debate, in various grades of dilemma, continues in Jewish communities today. Although most have a certain attachment to Israel, how many Jews who live outside Israel see themselves as exiles? More importantly, how many would be willing to use the term 'exile' of themselves?

A problem that became very clear in both the papers and the discussion was that we have no description of the actual process of deportation. There is in that sense no description of 'the exile'. There is also very little that claims to tell us about the resettled peoples and their life in their new location. Tobit tells the story of a Jew exiled by Shalmaneser to Nineveh. In that story Tobit sees himself as an exile from his native land, yet he is in no hurry to return to it, apparently because he knows of a further conquest and exile to come (Tob. 14.3-10). And yet there is little evidence that Jews of the later Second Temple period thought of themselves as exiles (Carroll, Grabbe, Davies). They looked to Jerusalem and the temple as some sort of religious centre and perhaps even as a place of eventual regathering, but this is rather different from thinking of oneself as being an exile. 'Diaspora' has a different nuance from 'exile'.

However, NPL partially disagrees with this assessment. He suggests that the distinction between 'exile' and 'diaspora' is artificial. The Hebrew word ($g\hat{o}l\hat{a}$) is the same in each case, meaning variously 'deportation', 'exile' and 'diaspora'. My point is slightly different, however, since it concerns concept rather than specific terminology. (A Jew like Philo and many others in the Greek diaspora would not have been using Hebrew, anyway.) I have seen no indication that diaspora Jews before 70 had a strong desire to settle in Palestine, in which case they would not have been 'exiles' in the strong sense of the word. Philip Davies makes the point that both those who returned and those who had a chance to return but did not, had given up any claim to be exiles—they had chosen to live elsewhere.

Evaluation of Sources and Historical Reconstruction

This was the most contentious issue in our first session, and the indications are that it remains so. There was a spectrum of views on this point. Perhaps one of the main differences was the extent to which it is legitimate to mix data from different sorts of sources. Using literary and archaeological data together was especially queried by Thompson. We would all insist that various sources need each to be considered in its own right before bringing them together. Far too often the archaeological has been interpreted by the literary and then the interpreted archaeological used to justify the literary, to produce a classic example of circular reasoning. Yet there are a number who would argue that one must bring together the archaeological and literary at some point (e.g. Jeppesen, Grabbe). It has been argued that in any case we would make no sense of the archaeological if we did not use the framework of the biblical text and other literary sources.[7] This argument for drawing on literary sources is purely a matter of methodological first principles—any such use must be careful and critical. It was also evident that the evaluation of particular sources covered a range of views. Rainer Albertz draws on the Neo-Babylonian sources in a way which few would find contentious, but these were more or less contemporaneous with the events that they profess to

7. Cf. J. Maxwell Miller, 'Is it Possible to Write a History of Israel without Relying on the Hebrew Bible?', in D.V. Edelman (ed.), *The Fabric of History: Text, Artifact and Israel's Past* (JSOTSup, 127; Sheffield: JSOT Press, 1991), pp. 93-102.

represent. As usual, the real crux is whether and to what extent the biblical text can be used. It is debated as to whether we have any archaeological evidence for the fall of Jerusalem in 587–586 BCE. However, it was argued that the biblical account of Judah's last few decades was sufficiently detailed and supported by external data that its version of the final siege and fall of Jerusalem could be accepted, even though there was no confirmatory evidence from about 594 BCE (Grabbe, Barstad). But this did not, and was not meant to be, a blanket argument for accepting the biblical text in other cases. On the contrary, no general statement could be made about the biblical text; each case had to be examined individually on its merits.

Another example was the description of the return as described in Ezra. It was asked (perhaps in a deliberately provocative manner) whether there was any reason to doubt Zerubbabel's return, the rebuilding of the temple about 520 BCE, and the like (EAK). Yet this information depends on the book of Ezra, and a number of those who would argue for use of the biblical text on some occasions were extremely sceptical of Ezra (e.g. Becking[8]). We know of Zerubbabel and the proposal to rebuild the temple from Haggai and Zechariah, but much of the information on the 'restoration' is found in the book of Ezra. If we do not accept the picture of Ezra, we are thrown back on trying to reconstruct what happened in the early Persian period from very fragmentary sources. Even on a fairly optimistic reading of Ezra, the dates given there are suspect, which makes the date for completion of the temple in 516 BCE difficult to affirm. We come back to the fact that we know nothing of the exile as such (except by analogy from Neo-Assyrian and other sources [Grabbe]) and depend to a large extent on the book of Ezra for the main events of the 'return' and 'restoration'. Without Ezra we are not entirely in the dark, since we have not only some data in Haggai and Zechariah but also the data from archaeology of Persian-period Yehud, but these do not tell us about the return from exile. Yet

8.   Bob Becking seems to have slightly misunderstood me in some of his comments on one of my articles; as far as I can see, I have taken much the same view as he does, most recently in *Ezra–Nehemiah* (Readings; London: Routledge, 1998). See also my earlier articles, 'Reconstructing History from the Book of Ezra', in P.R. Davies (ed.), *Second Temple Studies. I. The Persian Period* (JSOTSup, 117; Sheffield: JSOT Press, 1991), pp. 98-107; 'What Was Ezra's Mission?', in T.C. Eskenazi and K.H. Richards (eds.), *Second Temple Studies. II. Temple Community in the Persian Period* (JSOTSup, 175; Sheffield: JSOT, 1994), pp. 286-99.

would the biblical text have invented from whole cloth the concept of the return of some deportees? Is it legitimate to use scattered data to reconstruct a scenario in the early Persian period which includes the return of exiles?

Knud Jeppesen and Bob Becking argue that creating a narrative by reconstruction is a quite legitimate historical exercise, and this would be accepted by many within the Seminar.[9] Yet this is naturally a moot point. What sources is it legitimate to use and in what way? Perhaps the real question comes down to what the reconstructed narrative looks like and how it is to be used. Even more basically, to what extent can one use the biblical account? Hans Barstad's response puts a stark spotlight on what is still probably the most contentious issue among Seminar members: the place and use of the biblical literature.

Can a History of 'the Exile' Be Written?

The last question to be put to the Seminar participants was a difficult one to word without biasing the answer by the manner in which the question was asked. In an attempt to present a neutral question and to allow each participant to answer as he chose, I put the question rather broadly: 'Can a history of the "exile" (or of Judah and the Jews in the Neo-Babylonian period) be written? If so, what would it look like?' Many readers may be surprised at some of the answers, considering the remarks made earlier in the discussion or elsewhere in public or print.

RA: We have some data, but we cannot narrate a history. This is a dilemma I have to resolve because I am writing a book on the exile.[10]

BB: The answer is affirmative, but we would need to use our imagination to produce a (his)story out of the limited evidence. This implies that the (his)story would be of a tentative character and will remain open for debate. New evidence would be welcome.

9.   On this, see especially the discussion in Hans M. Barstad, 'History and the Hebrew Bible', in Grabbe (ed.), *Can a 'History of Israel' Be Written?*, pp. 37-64, in particular pp. 54-64.

10.   Rainer Albertz, *Die Exilszeit* (Biblische Enzyklopädie, 7; Stuttgart: W. Kohlhammer, forthcoming).

HMB: A short history can be written.

RPC: It would be an ideological history, using whatever data are available, but it would be a 'history' in quote marks.

PRD: There would be two histories. One would be of the idea of exile and its emergence in Judaism and Jewish literature, including the period up the rise of Zionism in the nineteenth century. The other would be of population movements of all sorts. The biblical literature could be fitted into the latter, but it would remain speculative to a lesser or greater extent.

LLG: I had already committed myself on this question in the conclusion of my paper where I stated that I thought such a history could be written, at least in a partial sense. We seem to have a good deal of information on the two decades preceding the fall of Jerusalem, giving reason to believe that the description of the fall of Jerusalem was more or less as described in the text. However, the bulk of the population was not deported but remained in Judah the whole time. Of the actual deportation, we have no information and can describe it only by analogy. The return from exile is almost as problematic. Although it seems evident that some descendants of the deportees returned, they did not return to an empty land. The temple was rebuilt, but precisely when is uncertain. Whether this is a 'history of the exile' or not, it is at least a (very brief) history of a particular period of time in the region of Judah.

KJ: There would be different sorts of history: both a shorter version, where the known historical facts from the period in question are listed and connected by means of only a few brief comments, and a longer one in which the gaps between the facts could be filled out with other sources such as the myth of exile. For example, the myth could be used to deal with the mentality of people in exile. Naturally, there could be more than one version of both the short and the long history.

EAK: A history of 20 to 200 pages could be written, depending on what sort of publication was envisaged. It would contain some clear historical dates, such as 609, 597, 586 and 582. It would include the boundaries of Yehud, the archaeology and destruction (or continuation) of specific sites, inscriptions. It would include the intellectual currents, discussion about language, Neo-Babylonian history (e.g. the reign of Nabonidus), and similar sorts of things.

NPL: Yes, a history can be written, but we must ask what kind of history. Would it be a history of the 'exile' as an intellectual experience or as plain history that happened once in the past? Here my view is not far from Philip Davies'.

TLT: Yes, a history could be written, but it would be based on archaeology and would take 300 pages to write.

Future Prospects

The subject of 'the exile' was hardly exhausted in either the papers or the discussion, but some of the main methodological issues were explored. The chosen subject thus served its purpose, and it was not felt that a further exploration of 'the exile' would advance the discussion significantly at this time. It is also important to make it clear that none of the Seminar members has said their 'last word' on the subject. Those who wrote papers had not seen the formal responses when they did the final revision.

The topic chosen for the Seminar's attention for the next two years is that of the Hellenistic period (meaning primarily the time from Alexander to the Maccabaean revolt). Focusing on it for two years will allow an investigation of an important period for both the literature and history of the Jews. Some of the questions to be considered are those of the editing and production of writings which became part of the Bible and others which did not but were still available to be adopted as authoritative writings,[11] Jewish historiography for this period and its implications for writing the history of the monarchial period and before, and the general milieu of this period which may have implications for history writing.

11. Cf. Niels Peter Lemche, 'The Old Testament—a Hellenistic Book', *SJOT* 7 (1993), pp. 163-93.

INDEXES

INDEX OF REFERENCES

BIBLICAL REFERENCES

OTHER ANCIENT REFERENCES

INDEX OF AUTHORS

JOURNAL FOR THE STUDY OF THE OLD TESTAMENT
SUPPLEMENT SERIES